More Index Card Games and Activities for ESL
▼

Other
Game Materials
available at
ProLinguaLearning.com

Index Card Games for ESL Index
Superphonic Bingo
The Great Big BINGO Book
Dictation Riddles
Shenanigames
The Dice Book

More Index Card Games and Activities
for ESL

Second Edition

Raymond C. Clark

PROLINGUA LEARNING

Pro Lingua Learning
PO Box 4467
Rockville, Maryland 20849 USA
Office: 301-424-8900
Orders: 800-888-4741
Email: info@ProLinguaLearning.com
Web: www.ProLinguaLearning.com

At Pro Lingua
our objective is to foster an approach
to learning and teaching that we call
interplay, *the* **inter**action *of language*
learners and teachers with their materials,
with the language and culture,
and with each other in active, creative,
and productive **play**.

Copyright © 1993, 2016, 2021 Raymond C. Clark

ISBN 13: 978-0-86647-370-5; 10: 0-86647-370-X

All rights reserved. No part of this publication may be reproduced or transmitted in any form or by any means, electronic, mechanical, photocopying, recording, or other, or stored in an information storage or retrieval system without permission in writing from the publisher. However, permission is granted by the publisher as follows:

Teachers may copy sample games for classroom use only.

The cover illustrations and those on pages 92, 109, and 126 to 128 are by Tyler Stiene. The portraits of the Presidents are Official White House Portraits used in *The ESL Miscellany*, 2015. The real estate photos and copy are adapted from a 2016 Vermont advertising pamphlet. Illustrations from Dreamstime.com Agency: page 81 © Destina156, pages 106-108 © Maxfx, page 162 © Ilynxv, pages 151-180 © Rtguest. The drawings on pages 129, 132, and 133 are by Patrick Moran. Information sources for Nations of the World: InfoPlease, Cities, 2014; UN Department of Economic and Social Affairs, World Bank, 2015.

This book was designed and set in Adobe Times New Roman by Arthur A. Burrows. This is a digital font based on an early twentieth century old-fashioned serif type called Times New Roman, commissioned by the British newspaper *The Times* in 1931 and designed by Victor Lardent for the Monotype company. Digitized and distributed with Microsoft products, it has become one of the most widely used typefaces in history. It is easy to read, with strong contrasting bold and italic faces. The book was printed and bound by Royal Palm Press in Punta Gorda, Florida.

Printed in the United States of America
Second, revised printing, second edition 2021.

Contents

Scrambled Sequences*   1

Story Cards   24

Cue Cards   38

Sort 'n' Stack   53

Improvicards   70

Correctocards   79

Quiz Cards*   90

Mime Cards   109

Conversocards   117

Instructocards   123

Pictograms**   130

Line-Ups   138

Finder Cards   159

* These activities can also be found in the original *Index Card Games for ESL*. The sample games in this book are different from those in the original.
** Pictograms is also included in *Teaching Languages for Communication and Accuracy*.

Acknowledgements

This second edition of *More Index Card Games and Activities for ESL* is obviously indebted to *Index Card Games for ESL,* Much of the historical information in this section comes from a special 1981 section of the Reformer, published on the occasion of the paper's moving from downtown Brattleboro to its headquarters on Black Mountain Road. compiled by teachers at the School for International Training, and first published in 1982. Since then I have continued to develop the collection, and in 1993, *More Index Card Games and Activities* was published. After several more years of creating and using index card games with graduate students at the School for International Training, Marlboro College's MATESL program, and the Southern New Hampshire University's MATEFL program at the University of Vietnam, I have finally revised and expanded the 1993 edition into this new edition. It has been a fun and challenging thirty-year project.

Introduction

The descriptions of how to make and use the various games and activities are self-explanatory, so there is no need in this introduction to belabor that point. However, for those of you who are not familiar with our previous books, let me point out that what you are now holding is basically a "cookbook" that tells you how to make and play the game. For each game/activitiy there are some samples to get you started. Please feel free to copy them, cut them out, and paste them on index cards – and if possible laminate them. My own collection now fills two large plastic bins.

RCC

More Index Card Games and Activities for ESL ▼

Scrambled Sequences

Brief Description

The students re-arrange a series of scrambled sentences. Each word is written on a separate card. To make the game easier, the first word can be capitalized and the punctuation can be included. First they unscramble a sentence.

computer	the	on.	First,	turn

First, turn the computer on.

In addition to each sentence being scrambled, there is a natural or logical sequence of scrambled sentences. For example, the sentence above is the first sentence in a three-sentence sequence.

First, turn the computer on.
Then find the mail icon.
Click on the icon.

The Complete Sequence (Each sentence is mixed up in a different envelope).

computer	The	on.	First,	turn
find	icon	mail	Then	the
icon.	Click	the	on	

Purpose

This game is useful for practicing and reviewing sentence word order and discourse markers (*first, then,* etc.) in a sequence or story.

Preparation

The game should have a natural or logical sequence of statements, such as instructions for checking your email.

Copy and cut up each sentence, making a collection of several words. Paste the words on index cards and put the cards for each sentence in a separate envelope.

Make at least 3 copies of each sentence. Thus, if there are 10 sentences in the sequence, you will need 30 envelopes. Write a number on each envelope. For example, if you have 3 copies of each sentence, the 3 sentences in their envelopes should have the same number.

The number of words in each sentence and the number of sentences in the sequence depends on the proficiency level of the students. As a rule of thumb,
>Beginner : 6 X 6 (six words in the sentence; six sentences in the sequence)
Intermediate: 8 x 8
Advanced: 12 x 12

Procedure

1. Divide the class into pairs or trios. Tell them the topic of the sequence.

2. Give each group two different envelopes. For example, if there are 5 pairs and each pair has 2 envelopes, if you have 30 envelopes, 20 extra envelopes are put in a central place.

3. Give each group a blank numbered list (see page 3).

4. When a group has solved a sentence, they write the sentence on a piece of paper. When they have solved all the sentences, they write them in the correct sequence using the blank list on page 3.

5. When they have finished their two sentences they return the envelopes to the central pile and take two more with different numbers.

6. Note that the sentences in the sample sequences are separated by darker lines.

Variations

1. For an easier activity, number the sentences according to their position in the sequence. Have the students write the sentences on the blank numbered list as they unscramble them.

TOPIC _____ TEAM _____

1. _____

2. _____

3. _____

4. _____

5. _____

6. _____

7. _____

8. _____

9. _____

10. _____

11. _____

12. _____

Sequence 1, Sending a Letter

Write	the	address
on	the	envelope.
Put	the	letter
in	the	envelope.
Seal	the	envelope.
Put	a	stamp
in	the	upper
right	corner.	Write
your	return	address
in	the	upper
left	corner.	

Sequence 2, Sharpening a Pencil

Find	the	pencil
sharpener.	Put	the
pencil	in	the
sharpener.	Turn	the
sharpener's	handle.	Continue
until	the	pencil
is	sharp.	Remove
the	pencil	from
the	sharpener.	

Sequence 3, Boiling Eggs

Fill	the	pot
with	water.	Heat
the	water	until
it	boils.	Put
the	eggs	in
the	water.	For
soft-boiled	eggs,	boil
three	minutes.	For
hard-boiled	eggs,	boil
five	minutes	

Sequence 4, Brushing Your Teeth

Take	the	cap
off	the	tube
of	toothpaste.	Squeeze
some	paste	onto
the	toothbrush.	Put
the	cap	back on
the	tube.	Brush
your	teeth	for
at least	two	minutes.
Rinse	your	mouth
and	your	toothbrush.

Sequence 5, Grocery Shopping

Get	a	shopping
cart	or	basket.
Put	your	reusable
shopping	bags	in
the	cart.	Pick
up	the	things
you	need.	Go
to	the	checkout
counter.	Pay	the
bill	and	go
home.		.

Sequence 6, Flying

Get	your	boarding pass
and	check	your
luggage.	Show	your
ID	and	boarding pass
and	go	through
security.	Take	everything
out of	your	pockets.
Go to	the	gate
and	wait.	Board
the	plane	when
it is	your	turn.

Sequence 7, Filling in a Form

Read	the	directions
at	the	top
of	the	form.
Write	your	name,
last	name	first.
Enter	your	address.
Give	your	date
of	birth.	Check
your	marital	status
and	your	educational
level.		

Sequence 7, Filling in a Form

Write	in	your
social security	and	driver's
license	numbers.	Sign
the	form.	
Write	today's	date.

Sequence 8, Starting a Car

Open	the	door
and	get	in.
Fasten	the	seat
belt.	Be	sure
the	car	is
in	park.	Insert
the	key.	

Sequence 8, Starting a Car

Turn	the	key
and	step	easily
on	the	gas
pedal.	Check	the
hand	brake.	Is
it	on?	Release
the	hand	brake.
Shift	into	drive
and	step	on
the	gas.	

Sequence 9, Using a Gas Pump

Drive	up	to
a	self-serve	pump.
Remove	the	gas
cap.	Choose	your
payment	option.	Select
the	grade	of
gas	you	want.

Put	the	nozzle
into	the	gas
tank.	Squeeze	the
handle	on	the
nozzle.	Release	the
handle	when	you
are	finished.	Return
the	hose	and
take	your	receipt.

Sequence 10, Cesar Chavez

Cesar	Chavez	was	born
in	1927	in	Arizona.
His	father	and	mother
were	farmers.	They	lost
their	home	because	of
a	terrible	drought.	They
had	to	travel	from
place	to	place	working
on	farms.	The	working
conditions	were	very	bad.
Cesar	decided	to	organize
the	workers.		

Sequence 10, Cesar Chavez

He	organized	strikes	and
fasted	for	better	conditions.
He	died	in	1993,
possibly	as	a	result
of	fasting.	He	was
awarded	the	Presidential	Medal
of	Freedom	in	1994.

Sequence 11, Emiliano Zapata

Until	1910	in	Mexico
a	few	families	owned
most	of	the	land.
Between	1910	and	1920
the	Mexican	Revolution	swept
the	country.	Emiliano	Zapata
became	a	leader	of
the	peasants.	In	Morelos,
Zapata	and	his	followers
took	over	the	land.

Sequence 11, Emiliano Zapata

The	President	of	Mexico
sent	an	army	to
Morelos.	He	wanted	to
capture	and	kill	Zapata.
The	Zapatistas	were	able
to	defend	their	land.
The	army	finally	killed
Zapata	in	an	ambush
in	1919.		

Sequence 12, Mother Jones

Mary	Harris	emigrated	from
Ireland	to	Canada.	Mary
moved	to	the	United
States	and	married	George
Jones.	She	lost	her
husband	and	her	four
children	to	the	yellow
fever	epidemic	of	1867.
In	the	great	Chicago
fire	of	1871	she
lost	everything	she	owned.
After	these	misfortunes,	she

Sequence 12, Mother Jones

got	a	job	with
a	labor	union.	Mary
saw	that	the	owners
of	factories	and	mines
were	abusing	their	employees.
She	organized	the	workers
and	protested	the	working
conditions.	She	was	put
in	jail,	but	she
never	stopped	working	for
better	working	conditions.	

Sequence 13, The Origin of the Big Dipper — *Fox Indian tale*

One day three men decided to hunt for Bear.	When they found Bear's cave, their dog, Hold Tight, chased Bear out.
The hunters tried to shoot Bear. but it was too fast.	Bear ran north and the hunters chased Bear.
Finally one of the hunters looked back.	"Oh no," he shouted. "Bear is leading us up into the sky."
They tried to turn around and get down.	It was too late; they were trapped.
You can see them today.	The four stars in a square are Bear.
The three stars behind Bear are the hunters and the tiny star is Hold Tight.	

Sequence 14, Bear, Ant, and Yellowjacket

Coastal Salish Indian tale

Bear, Ant, and Yellowjacket were arguing about how long day should be.	Bear liked to sleep so he wanted day and night to each be six months long.
Ant and Yellowjacket wanted day and night to be much shorter.	They wanted many days and nights in a year.
They decided to have a race, and the winner would decide the length of the day and night.	They began the race, and Bear quickly took the lead.
Yellowjacket finally caught up with Bear and began to sting him.	Bear was confused and climbed up a tree.
Meanwhile Ant raced on ahead and won the race.	That is why we have many days and nights in a year.
However, Bear is still angry because Ant and Yellowjacket tricked him.	And that is why Bear tears up the nests of Ant and Yellowjacket whenever he finds them.

Story Cards

Brief Description

On each card there is a short, complete narrative text. The students read and study the texts and then try to tell the stories in their own words without looking at the cards.

Purpose

To give the students practice in giving various types of short narrations. The card contains the basic text from which the students get the information and to which they can later refer, comparing their version to the original. The narration also provides practice in extended discourse and discourse markers such as *then, next,* and *finally*.

Preparation

There are several different kinds of potential narrations, from telling folktales to reciting encyclopedic information. After choosing the type you wish to work on (see Suggestions), and after finding the material, you may need to abridge and edit the text. If so, keep the following in mind:

1. For beginning level students, sentence length can be critical. Sentences of 8-10 words are sufficiently challenging. Intermediate students can cope with sentences of up to 20 words, and advanced students can work with sentences of more than 20 words.

2. Grammatical constructions also need to be controlled. Consult a pedagogical grammar for ideas. In general, simple sentences with single subjects, short, active voice verb phrases, and single objects will be necessary at the beginning level. Compound sentences, sentences joined by *and* or *but* are possible at the intermediate level, along with short noun phrases (*my dear old friend*) and clauses (I know *(that) my friend will help you*). Complex sentences with subordinate adverbial clauses introduced by *because, although, if,* or *after* can be introduced at the intermediate level. Relative clauses can also be tricky.

3. The vocabulary may need to be edited. Consult a word frequency list to get an idea of which words can and should be dealt with at the beginning level. Also keep in mind your own knowledge of your students' vocabulary level and try to choose and prepare texts that have only a few new or unusual words. The purpose of this activity is not vocabulary expansion, but rather, discourse fluency.

Procedure

1. Give each student a different card. Ask them to read and study their cards. Tell them to note vocabulary that is both unfamiliar and central to the narration.

2. Collect the vocabulary from the students and go over definitions with the whole class. One effective way of doing this is to have the students put their words on the board after they have finished studying their cards. You can leave the words on the board throughout steps 3 and 4.

3. Pair off the students. Have them try to tell each other the texts of their cards without looking at them. After they have shared their stories, they should look again at their cards to compare what they have just said with what is on the card.

4. The pairs split up and find new partners to share their stories with. One purpose of the repetition is for the students to improve their performance with each telling, so that they become fluent and accurate. This step can be repeated several times, probably for a maximum of 6 times. Although it is repetitive for the tellers, they also get to hear several different stories.

Variations

1. After exchanging stories, the students can also exchange cards, split up, practice a bit, and tell the story they just heard to another person.

2. The students can also work in groups of three to six, so that they have practice telling stories to more than one person at a time.

3. The students can also tell their stories to the entire class. You could do this as a one-a-day activity.

4. You or a student can read the story as a listening/dictation exercise.

5. You can tell the story deliberately once through as the students take notes. They then write the story and compare it with the original, which you can post, read again, or hand out.

Suggestions

*1. Folktales and fables.

*2. Jokes or anecdotes.

3. Movie reviews. Video guidebooks have thousands of short summaries.

*4. Brief bio-sketches.

5. Famous events such as the Wright Brothers' flight, or the sinking of the *Titanic*.

6. Short news articles.

7. Weather reports from around the world, or local ones from different times of the year.

8. Mother Goose rhymes.

*9. Limericks.

10. Plots of famous stories from Shakespeare, the Brothers Grimm, Hans Christian Andersen, Greek mythology.

11. Horoscopes.

12. Holidays.

* *See sample games on the following pages.*

Story Cards — Aesop's Fables

The Fox and the Boar

The fox passed by the boar, who was busily sharpening his tusks on a tree. "Why are you doing that now?" asked the fox. "There is no enemy anywhere near here." The boar answered, "You are right, my friend, but when the enemy is near, it will be too late."

The Fox and the Grapes

One day a hungry fox saw some beautiful grapes. They were hanging in great bunches from the vine. But they were high above the ground. The fox jumped and jumped to reach them, but he could not. Angrily he walked away and said, "They may look beautiful, but I am sure that inside they are sour."

The Hare and the Hound

A hunting dog found a nice hare in the field. Immediately he began to chase the hare. But the hare was an excellent runner, and in a short time the hound gave up, breathless. The hound's master came up to the hound and teased the tired dog because he had failed. "Master," said the hound, "you may laugh, but consider that he was running for his life, while I was running only for your dinner."

The Crow and the Pitcher

A thirsty crow found a pitcher with water in it. But the pitcher's neck was narrow and the crow's beak could not reach the water. He tried to turn the pitcher over, but it was too heavy. So he patiently gathered pebbles from the ground and dropped them one by one into the pitcher. This caused the water to reach the top, and so he got his drink.

Story Cards   *Aesop's Fables*

The Bird, the Beasts, and the Bats

Once there was a fierce war between the birds and the beasts. The bats at first fought with the birds, but the battle went badly for the birds. And so the bats joined the beasts. Thanks to the mighty eagle, the birds began to win. The bats, in shame, left the field of battle to spend their days in caves, coming out only at night when the birds had gone to roost.

The Shepherd Boy and the Wolf

A young shepherd boy became bored with his work. One day he cried, "Wolf! Wolf!" to see what would happen. All the people working in the field ran to help, but there was no wolf. The young shepherd was very pleased with all the excitement. A few days later he did it again, but the people who came were not amused. The next day, a wolf came. The boy cried, "Wolf! Wolf!" but nobody came, and the wolf enjoyed a fine meal.

The Oak and the Reeds

A proud and tall oak tree grew beside a stream. It looked down on the thin and lowly reeds growing by the side of the stream. One day a violent wind blew the oak into the stream. The oak saw the reeds were still standing, and asked them how they had escaped the storm. "We bent our heads," they said, "while you stood stiff and stubborn."

The Ants and the Grasshopper

The grasshopper sang and sang all the summer. But as winter came he began to be hungry. So he went to the door of the ants who lived nearby. He asked them to give him a little food. "I shall pay next summer," he said. "And what did you do *this* summer?" asked the ants. "Oh, I sang all day," answered the grasshopper. "Well then, now you can dance," said the ants, and they closed the door.

Story Cards *Aesop's Fables*

The Dog and the Reflection

One day a dog stole a piece of meat. Happily he ran home until he came to a small stream, which was bridged by a low plank. As he crossed, he saw another dog in the water with a big piece of meat in his mouth. Greedily he snapped at the other dog's meat, but of course his own piece of meat fell from his mouth and floated down the stream.

The Horse and the Donkey

A fat and lazy horse was traveling with a heavily loaded donkey, in the company of their master. The donkey, whose back was early breaking, begged the horse to help carry the load. But the proud horse refused A little farther along the road, the donkey fell down and died. The master then threw the load on the horse's back and on top of that, the dead donkey.

The Goat and the Wolf

One day a goat saw a dangerous wolf coming toward him. Now, the goat is an excellent rock climber and there was a high rock nearby. So he climbed the rock, knowing the wolf could not follow. From the safety of his position he cursed and teased the wolf. The wolf looked up and said, "Don't think that you annoy me. I know your bad language comes from the rock you are standing on, and not from you."

The Old Man and Death

A poor and tired peasant staggered along a lonely and dusty road. On his shoulders he carried a heavy load of wood for his fire. At last he dropped the load, unable to continue. Sitting upon it, he thought how cruel life was. From dawn to dark, work and more work. He called on Death to free him. Suddenly, Death appeared and asked him what he wanted. "Nothing," said the man. "Just help me place this load back on my shoulders."

Story Cards

Aesop's Fables

The Horse and the Stag

The horse and the stag, two wild forest friends, quarreled. Angered, the horse went to a man and begged the man to help him get revenge against the stag. The man agreed and saddled the horse. Together they rode after the stag and killed it. Joyfully, the horse thanked his rider and asked him to remove the saddle. "Oh no," said the man. "Now I see how valuable and useful you are." And from then on, the horse lost his freedom and served man.

The Boar and the Donkey

The boar and the donkey got into an argument, and the boar with his long tusks decided to challenge the tuskless donkey to a fight. The time for battle came and the two approached each other. Then, with a great roar, the boar lowered his head and charged. The donkey suddenly turned around and kicked the boar in the face. The boar staggered, falling to the ground, and said, "Who would have expected an attack from that end?"

The Blackbird and the Doves

A blackbird saw that the white doves lived in a fine house. They ate well and they seemed very happy together. He decided to join them, so he whitened his feathers. One evening he entered the doves' house unnoticed. After a short while he began to feel very proud of his trick, and he laughed aloud. The doves instantly beat him and drove him out of the house. Sadly he returned to his former mates, but when they saw this strange white bird, they too drove him away.

The Tortoise and the Hare

The hare loved to tease the tortoise about his slowness. One day, the tortoise challenged the hare to a race. The hare, thinking this was a great joke, agreed. The fox was selected to be the judge. The race began, and of course, the hare left the tortoise far behind. At the midpoint, the hare decided to take a little nap in the gentle sun. He knew he could easily win even if the tortoise caught up. The sun sank low, and the hare awoke with a start to see night approaching. He raced to the finish line to find the fox and the tortoise waiting.

Story Cards *Bio-Sketches: Heroes*

Queen Victoria

Queen Victoria was born in 1819. She became Queen of England in 1837. She married her cousin, Prince Albert, whom she loved very deeply. They had nine children whose marriages led to alliances with Russia, Germany, Greece, Denmark, and Romania. During her time England became a world power as an industrial and imperialist nation. She died in 1901 after a reign of almost 64 years.

Ramon Magsaysay

Ramon Magsaysay was born in 1907. From 1950 to 1953, he was secretary for national defense for the Republic of the Philippines. In this position, he reformed the army and crushed the communist-supported Huk rebels. From 1953 to 1957 he served as president of the Philippines. He followed a policy of close cooperation with the U.S. He was killed in an airplane crash in 1957.

Eva Peron

Eva Peron (Evita) was born in 1919. She was an actress when she met and later married Juan Peron in 1945. When Peron became President of Argentina in 1946, Eva became a powerful member of his government. In effect, she was the minister of health and labor. She was a spokesperson for women's rights, labor, and the poor. The army blocked her from the position of vice president in 1951. She died the following year of cancer, at the age of 33.

Story Cards *Bio-Sketches: Heroes*

José de San Martín

José de San Martín was born in 1778. He was a South American revolutionary. In 1812 he took part in Argentina's revolution against Spain. Then he led the army across the Andes Mountains into Chile, where he brought the Chilean revolution to a successful conclusion. He next entered Peru, but after meeting with Simón Bolívar, who had entered Peru from the north, he left Peru and retired to private life. He died in 1850.

David Ben-Gurion

David Ben-Gurion was born in Poland in 1886. He settled in Palestine in 1906. He became an active Zionist, but during World War I, he supported the British. During World War II, he again cooperated with the British, but after the war he turned against them to lead the Israeli fight for nationhood. He became the first prime minister of Israel in 1948. He was in and out of office until 1963, when, as prime minister, he retired. However, he remained active in politics until his death in 1973.

Gamal Abdel Nasser

Gamal Abdel Nasser was born in 1918 in Alexandria, Egypt. As a young student, he was expelled from school for protests against the British. He graduated from the Egyptian Royal Military Academy in 1938. Ten years later he founded the secret Society of Free Officers. In 1952 he led a coup that deposed King Farouk, and in 1956 he became president of Egypt. Despite a military defeat in 1967 at the hands of Israel, he was a very popular leader. He died in 1970.

Story Cards *Bio-Sketches: Heroes*

Queen Cleopatra

Cleopatra was born in 69 B.C. She was the daughter of Ptolemy XI. She was married to her brother Ptolemy XII, who drowned in the Nile, and then to a younger brother, Ptolemy XIII. During her second marriage, she was the mistress of Julius Caesar. She bore him a son. After Caesar's death, Marc Antony visited her and fell in love with her. They planned to build an empire, but their armies were defeated by Octavian. Antony committed suicide, and Cleopatra allowed an asp to bite her. She died in 30 B.C. at the age of 39.

Joan of Arc

Joan of Arc was born around 1412, the daughter of a farmer. As a teenager she began to hear voices that told her to help Charles VII. She put on men's clothes and managed to convince Charles to give her soldiers. She achieved several victories, beginning with Orleans. In 1429 she stood beside Charles when he was proclaimed king of France. She continued her military career against the English and their allies, the Burgundians, but she was captured, tried, and burned at the stake in 1431.

Atatürk

Mustafa Kemal (Atatürk) the founder of modern Turkey, was born in 1880 in Thessaloniki, Greece. He chose a military career in the Turkish army. During World War I, he defeated the Europeans at Gallipoli and became a national hero. As Turkey collapsed at the end of World War I, Atatürk set up a new government in Ankara. Throughout 1921-1922 he led the Turkish army into victory over the Europeans. He served four terms as the first president of modern Turkey. He carried out many reforms in his drive to westernize Turkey. He died in 1938.

Story Cards *Bio-Sketches: Heroes*

Benito Juárez

Benito Juárez was born in 1806 in Oaxaca and is the only full-blooded Indian to ever be president of Mexico. He became governor of the state of Oaxaca, but in 1853, because of his criticism of the government, he went into exile in New Orleans, where he worked in a cigar factory. Juárez returned to Mexico in 1855 as minister of justice. The Juárez Law of 1855 declared all citizens equal before the law and severely restricted the privileges of the Catholic Church and the military. In 1858 Juárez became President of Mexico. He died at his desk from a heart attack in 1872.

Eleanor Roosevelt

Eleanor Roosevelt was born in 1884. Her childhood was difficult, as both her parents and her brother died by the time she was 10 years old. She then went to live with her grandmother. Eleanor married Franklin Roosevelt, her fifth cousin, and supported his long career as a politician and President of the United States. She was very active in politics and social issues. When her husband died she continued to work for many causes, such as human rights and the status of women, and she pressed the United States to support the United Nations.

Florence Nightingale

Florence Nightingale was a pioneer of modern nursing. She was born in 1820 in the city of Florence, Italy. In 1844 she decided to enter the field of nursing. Her wealthy parents were very upset, because they thought this was not a proper career for an upper-class woman. In 1853 she served as a nurse for the British army in Istanbul during the Crimean War. She became famous for reporting on the horrible conditions in the hospital. She went back to England and promoted the importance of good sanitation. In 1860 she established a professional nursing school. It was the first secular nursing school in the world. She died in 1910 at the age of 90.

Story Cards *Bio-Sketches: Heroes*

Indira Gandhi

Indira Gandhi was born in Allahabad, India in 1917. Her father, Jawharlal Nehru, was the first Prime Minister of India. She herself became the third Prime Minister in 1966. She was educated in Switzerland and in England, where she attended Oxford University. When her mother died in 1936, Indira became active as her father's hostess, meeting many world leaders. During her years as Prime Minister she ruled with a strong hand. When a Sikh separatist movement developed, she sent the army to the Sikh's Golden Temple. As a result many people died. On October 31, 1984, her trusted Sikh bodyguards assassinated her.

Nelson Mandela

Nelson Mandela was born in 1918, in Transkei, South Africa. In his 20s he began to work against the apartheid policies of South Africa that segregated the races and promoted white supremacy. In 1942 he joined the African National Congress and for 20 years defied the South African government in peaceful, non-violent ways. In 1961 he began to doubt the non-violent approach. He began to feel that an armed struggle was necessary. He was arrested for leading a strike. In 1963 he was sentenced to life in prison. After 27 years in prison he was released. He began working with President F.W. de Klerk to dismantle apartheid. For their work they were awarded the Nobel Peace Prize in 1993. Mandela died at the age of 95 in 2013.

Benazir Bhutto

Benazir Bhutto was born in Karachi, Pakistan, in 1953. At the age of 16 she attended Radcliffe College of Harvard University. She graduated with a B.A. in 1973. From 1973 to 1977 she studied at Oxford University. During those years, her father, Zulfikar Ali Bhutto, was Prime Minister of Pakistan. However, he was deposed by a military coup, and in 1979 he was hanged. Benazir was arrested many times for her protests against the government, and finally in 1984 she left Pakistan for London. In 1986 she was back in Pakistan, and at age 35 was elected Prime Minister. Thereafter she was in and out of office, and in 1999 went into exile in Dubai. She returned once more in 2008, but was assassinated while campaigning for office.

Story Cards *Limericks*

There was an old man of Blackheath
Who sat on his set of false teeth.
  Said he with a start,
  "Oh Lord, bless my heart,
I have bitten myself underneath!"
	There was a young lady from Crete,
	Who was so exceedingly neat,
	  When she got out of bed,
	  She stood on her head
	To make sure of not soiling her feet.

As a beauty, I'm not a star,
There are many more handsome by far;
  But my face, I don't mind it
  For I am behind it,
It's the people in front get a jar.
	There once was a man from Calcutta
	Who spoke with a terrible stutter.
	  At breakfast he said,
	  "Give me some some b-bread
	And b-b-b-b-b-b-butter."

There was a young lady of Crewe
Who wanted to catch the 2:02.
  Said a porter, "Don't worry,
  Or hurry or scurry,
It's a minute or two to 2:02.
	A greedy old hoodlum named Harry
	Stole more than he really could carry.
	  With no room in his sack
	  Nor in his backpack,
	In the garden the loot Harry buried.

A thrifty young fellow of Shoreham
Made brown paper trousers and wore 'em.
  He looked nice and neat
  Till he bent in the street,
To pick up a coin; then he tore 'em.
	A painter who lived in Great Britain
	Interrupted two girls at their knittin'.
	  Said he with a sigh,
	  "That park bench did I
	Paint right where you two have been sittin'."

There once was a boy from Baghdad,
An inquisitive sort of lad.
  He said, "Let us see
  If a sting has a bee,"
And he very soon found that it had.
	Despite her impressive physique,
	Fatima was really quite meek;
	  If a mouse showed its head,
	  She would jump into bed
	With a terrible blood-curdling shriek.

A housewife called out with a frown,
When surprised by some callers from town:
  "In a minute or less,
  I'll slip on a dress –"
But she slipped on the stairs and fell down.
	A Korean whose home was in Seoul,
	Had notions uncommonly droll;
	  He'd got himself stewed
	  And posed in the nude
	On top of a telephone pole.

Story Cards *Limericks*

There was a young man from Tacoma
Whose breath had a whiskey aroma;
    To alter the smell
    He swallowed Chanel
And went off in a heavenly coma.
	A flea and a fly in a flue
	Were imprisoned, so what could they do?
	    Said the fly, "Let us flee!"
	    Said the flea, "Let us fly!"
	So they flew through a flaw in the flue.

There was a young fellow of Ceuta
(SAI OOTA)
Who rode into church on his scooter.
    He knocked down the dean .
    And said, "Sorry, old bean!
I ought to have sounded my hooter."
	There once was a spaceman named Wright,
	Whose speed was much faster than light.
	    He set out one day
	    In a relative way
	And returned on the previous night!

A dentist who lives in Duluth
Has wedded a widow named Ruth,
    Who is so sentimental
    Concerning things dental,
She calls her dear Second her Twoth.
	A young rock-and-roller named Clyde
	Always kept his guitar by his side.
	    All night he was strumming
	    And never stopped humming
	Till he ran out of rhythm and died.

There was a young parson called Perkins
Exceedingly fond of small gherkins.
    One summer at tea,
    He ate forty-three,
Which pickled his internal workin's.
	An old maid, a foolish romantic,
	Said as she crossed the Atlantic,
	    "Now is my chance
	    To find true romance
	On this beautiful ship, the *Titanic*."

You will find by the banks of the Nile
The home of the great crocodile.
    He will welcome you in
    With an innocent grin
Which gives way to a satisfied smile.
	A tutor who tooted the flute
	Tried to tutor two tooters to toot.
	    Said the two to the tutor,
	    "Is it harder to toot or
	To tutor two tooters to toot?

When the twins came their father, Dan Dunne,
Gave Edward as name to each son.
    When folks cried "Absurd!"
    He replied, "Ain't you heard
That two Eds are better than one?"
	A silly young man named Bill Beebee
	Was in love with a lady named Phoebe.
	    "But," said he, "I must see
	    What the marriage fee be
	Before Phoebe be Phoebe Beebee.

Cue Cards

Brief Description

Each student has a card containing factual information that is not in sentence form. The student must carry on a conversation with a partner using the information on the card.

Purpose

To provide a limited context/situation/topic within which two learners can practice giving and receiving information in sentences, i.e. semi-controlled conversation practice.

Preparation

Choose a topic that lends itself to building a collection of similar cards. See the list of *Suggestions* for ideas. Then conduct some research to collect information that can be put on the cards. The amount and kind of information will be influenced by the proficiency level of the students. It would be possible to make up to three sets of cards (easy, intermediate, difficult) in one topical area. Obviously, easy cards would have only a few pieces of information that would require simple questions and answers, for example, *What is the population of your country?* The number of different cards would depend on how many students you have in your class. The bare minimum would be one different card for each student. You could also build a number of different sets all at the same proficiency level and in the same topical area.

Procedure

1. Go over the types of information on the cards and the names for the various categories. For example, the students should understand the meaning of "literacy" before they begin the information exchange on "Nations of the World."

2. You may want to go over and put on the board, or poster paper, the types of questions and answers that would normally be used in giving and getting information. You could say, for example, "How do I find out about a country's location?" and as the students contribute questions you write them down. In this case a legitimate question would be *Where is your country located?* And a typical answer would be *My country is located* _____.

3. Give each student a card and allow them to study it for a few minutes. Circulate and be available for questions. If everybody is asking you the same question, you may need to interrupt and go over the question with the group.

4. Pair off the students. If there is an odd number, you can work with one student or you can set up a trio. The students ask and answer questions, or simply tell each other the information on the card. Intermediate or advanced students can discuss the information on the card.

5. Similar to the *Story Cards* procedure, when a pair has successfully completed their exchange, they break up and find new partners and do another information exchange. Each student keeps their own card, thus repeating the information with the new partner (and doing it more fluently), and hearing new information.

Variations

1. Groups of three, four, five, or even larger can be formed to give and take information.

2. Students can carry on conversations based on the information on the cards, rather than simple information questions (WH questions). For example, a student might say, *Oh, I've been in your country.*

3. Using the basic information on the card, the students can do additional research and give oral reports to the entire class. The reports can be spaced out, one a day over several days.

4. The information can be used as the basis for a short writing assignment.

5. You, or a student, can give a brief dictation with the information on the card.

Suggestions

 *1. Nations of the world (*Sources*: Infoplease, World Bank)
  2. Cities of the world
  3. States of the U.S.; provinces of Canada
 *4. Presidents of the U.S.
  5. Bio-sketches (facts only; not in paragraph form as in *Story Cards*)
  6. Personal résumés
  7. Timelines of various kinds
 *8. Real estate listings
  9. Classified ads
 10. Animal facts
 11. This day in history
 12. Types of automobiles, planes, ships
 13. Baseball or other trading cards

Included on the following pages

Cue Cards *Nations of the World*

Afghanistan

Capital: Kabul
Area: 250,000 sq mi
Population: 32,006,800 (40th*)
Largest Cities: Kabul 3,097,000;
  Kandahar 349,300;
  Mazari-Sharif 246,900
Languages: Dari, Pashtu
Ethnicity: Pashtun 42%, Tajik 27%,
  Hazara 9%, Uzbek 9%
Religions: Sunni Muslim 80%,
  Shi'a Muslim 19%
Literacy Rate: 28.1%
Currency: Afghani

Brazil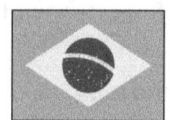

Capital: Brasilia
  (Population 3,789,000)
Area: 3,265,000 sq mi
Population: 203,657,200 (5th*)
Largest Cities: Sao Paulo 19,900,000;
  Rio de Janeiro 11,836,000;
  Salvador 2,594,000
Life Expectancy: 72.8 yrs
Languages: Portuguese
Ethnicity: White 53.7%, Mulatto (White
  & Black) 38.5%, Black 6.2%
Religions: Roman Catholic 74%,
  Protestant 15%
Literacy Rate: 88.6%
Currency: Real

Argentina

Capital: Buenos Aires
Area: 1,056,636 sq mi
Population: 42,152,900 (32nd*)
Largest Cities: Buenos Aires 13,528,000;
  Córdoba 1,556,000; Rosario 1,283,000
Life Expectancy: 77.1 yrs
Languages: Spanish (official), English,
  Italian, German, French
Ethnicity: White Spanish and Italian 97%
Religions: Roman Catholic 92%,
  Protestant 2%, Jewish 2%
Literacy Rate: 97.2%
Currency: Peso

China

Capital: Beijing
Area: 3,600,900 sq mi
Population: 1,401,586,600 (1st*)
Largest Cities: Shanghai 20,208,000;
  Beijing 15,594,000;
  Guangzhou 10,849,000
Life Expectancy: 74.4 yrs
Languages: Mandarin, Cantonese, Wu,
  Minbei
Ethnicity: Han Chinese 91.5%,
  Others 8.5%
Religions: Officially Atheist, Daoist,
  Buddhist, Christian 3-4%,
  Muslim 1-2%
Literacy Rate: 92.2%
Currency: Yuan/Renminbi

* World ranking by population

Cue Cards *Nations of the World*

Colombia

Capital: Bogota
Area: 401,042 sq mi
Population: 45,529, 200 (28th*)
Largest Cities: Bogota 8,743,000; Medellin 3,497,800; Cali 2,232,000
Life Expectancy: 74.8 yrs
Languages: Spanish
Ethnicity: Mestizo 58%, White 20%, Mulatto 14%, Black 4%
Religions: Roman Catholic 90%
Literacy Rate: 92.2%
Currency: Colombian Peso

Egypt

Capital: Cairo
Area: 384,344 sq mi
Population: 84,705,800 (15th*)
Largest Cities: Cairo 11,169,000; Alexandria 4,394,000; Giza 2,597,600
Life Expectancy: 72.9 yrs
Languages: Arabic
Ethnicity: Egyptian 98%,
Religions: Muslim (mosty Sunni) 90%, Coptic Christian 9%, other Christian 1 %
Literacy Rate: 71.4%
Currency: Egyptian Pound

Cuba

Capital: Havana
Area: 42,800 sq mi
Population: 11,248,750 (77th*)
Largest Cities: Havana 2,116,000; Santiago de Cuba 554,400; Camaguey 354,400
Life Expectancy: 77.9 yrs
Languages: Spanish
Ethnicity: Mulatto 51%, White 37%, Black 11%
Religions: Roman Catholic
Literacy Rate: 99.8%
Currency: Cuban Peso

Greece

Capital: Athens
Area: 50,502 sq mi
Population: 11,125,830 (80th*)
Largest Cities: Athens 3,414,000, Thessaloniki 883,000
Life Expectancy: 80.05 yrs
Languages: Greek 99%
Ethnicity: Greek 93%
Religions: Greek Orthodox 98%
Literacy Rate: 99.8%
Currency: Euro (formerly Drachma)

* World ranking by population

Cue Cards *Nations of the World*

India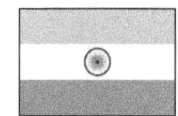

Capital: New Delhi
Area: 1,147,949 sq mi
Population: 1,282,390,303 (2nd*)
Largest Cities: New Delhi 22,654,000.
  Mumbai 19,744,000,
  Kolkata 14,402,000
Life Expectancy: 67.1 yrs
Languages: Hindi 41%, Bengali 8%,
  Telugu 7.2%, Marathi 7% Tamil 5.9%,
  Urdu 5%
Ethnicity: Indo-Aryan 72%,
  Dravidian 25%, Mongoloid
  and other 3%
Religions: Hindu 80.5%, Muslim 13.4%,
  Christian 2.3% Sikh 1.9% Others 1.9%
Literacy Rate: 61%
Currency: Rupee

Iran

Capital: Tehran
Area: 631,659 sq mi
Population: 78,470,200 (17th*)
Largest Cities: Tehran 7,304,000;
  Mashhad 2,713,000; Esfahan 1,781,000
Life Expectancy: 70.4 yrs
Languages: Persian 53%, Azeri Turk
  and Turkic dialects 18%, Kurdish 10%
Ethnicity: Persian 61%,
  Azerbaijani 16%, Kurd 10%. Arab 2%
Religions: Muslim 98% (Shi'a 89%,
  Sunni 9%)
Literacy Rate: 77%
Currency:: Rial

Indonesia

Capital: Jakarta
Area: 699,548 sq mi
Population: 252,812,250 (4th*)
Largest Cities: Jakarta 9,769,000;
  Surabaya 2,787,000;
  Bandung 2,429,000
Life Expectancy: 71.6 yrs
Languages: Bahasa Indonesia
Ethnicity: Javanese 40.6%,
  Sundanese 15%, Madurese 3.3 %; Others
Religions: Muslim 86.1%,
  Protestant 5.7%, Roman Catholic 3%,
  Hindu 1.8%
Literacy Rate: 90.4%
Currency: Rupiah

Japan

Capital: Tokyo
Area: 140,728 sq mi
Population: 126,818,000 (10th*)
Largest Cities: Tokyo 37,217,000;
  Osaka-Kobe 11,494,000;
  Nagoya 3,328,000
Life Expectancy: 83.9 yrs
Languages: Japanese
Ethnicity: Japanese 98.5%
  Korean 0.5%, Chinese 0.4%
Religions: Shintoism 83.9%,
  Buddhism 71.4%, Christian 2%
Literacy Rate: 99 %
Currency: Yen

* World ranking by population

Cue Cards — Nations of the World

Mexico

Capital: Mexico City
Area: 742,485 sq mi
Population: 123,799,200 (11th*)
Largest Cities: Mexico City 20,446,000; Guadalajara 4,525,000; Monterey 4,213,000; Puebla 2,335,000.
Life Expectancy: 76.2 yrs
Languages: Spanish
Ethnicity: Mestizo 60%, Amerindian 30%, White 9%
Religions: Roman Catholic 89%, Protestant 6%
Literacy Rate: 91 %
Currency: Mexican Peso

Pakistan

Capital: Islamabad
Area: 300,664 sq mi
Population: 185, 132, 900 (6th*)
Largest Cities: Karachi 13,876,000, Lahore 7,566,000; Faisalabad 3,038,000
Life Expectancy: 65.3 yrs
Languages: Urdu 8% (official), Punjabi 48%, Sindhi 12%, Pashtu 8%, Balochi 3%, English
Ethnicity: Punjabi, Sindhi, Pashtun, Baloch, Muhajir
Religions: Muslim 97% (Sunni 77%, Shi'a 20%) Christian, Hindu
Literacy Rate: 49.9 %
Currency: Pakistani Rupee

Nigeria

Capital: Abuja
Area: 351,649 sq mi
Population: 183,523,430 (7th*)
Largest Cities: Lagos 11, 223,000; Kano 3,375,900; Ibadan 2,949,000
Life Expectancy: 47.2 yrs
Languages: English (official), Hausa, Yoruba, Igbo, Fulani, 200 others
Ethnicity: Hausa and Fulani 29%, Yoruba 21%, Igbo 18%, Ijaw 10%, Others 22%
Religions: Muslim 50%, Christian 40%, Indigenous 10%
Literacy Rate: 68 %
Currency: Naira

Russia

Capital: Moscow
Area: 6,592,812 sq mi
Population: 142,088,100 (9th*)
Largest Cities: Moscow 11,621,000; St, Petersburg 4,866,000; Novosibirsk 1,478,000
Life Expectancy: 66.5 yrs
Languages: Russian, many minority languages
Ethnicity:: Russian 79.8%, Tatar 3.8%, Ukrainian 2%, Others
Religions:a Russian Orthodox 15-20%, Other Christian 2% , Muslim 10-15%
Literacy Rate: 99.4 %
Currency: Ruble

* World ranking by population

Cue Cards *Nations of the World*

Saudi Arabia

Capital: Riyadh
Area: 829,995 sq mi
Population: 29,369,400 (44th*)
Largest Cities: Riyadh 5,451,000; Jeddah 3,578,000; Makkah 1,591,000
Life Expectancy: 74.4 yrs
Languages: Arabic
Ethnicity: Arab 90%, Afro-Asian 10%
Religions: Muslim 100%
Literacy Rate: 78.8% %
Currency: Riyal

South Korea

Capital: Seoul
Area: 37,421 sq mi
Population: 49,750,230 (27th*)
Largest Cities: Seoul 9,736,000; Busan 3,372,000; Inchon 2,622,000
Life Expectancy: 79.3 yrs
Languages: Korean
Ethnicity: Korean 99.99 %
Religions: None 49.3%, Christian 26.3% (Protestant 19,7%, Catholic 6.6%), Buddhists 23.2%
Literacy Rate: 98 %
Currency: Won

Senegal

Capital: Dakar
Area: 74,131 sq mi
Population: 14,967,450 (72nd*)
Largest Cities: Dakar 3,035,000
Life Expectancy: 60.2 yrs
Languages: French (official), Wolof, Pulaar, Jola, Mandika
Ethnicity: Wolof 43,3%, Fulani 23,8%, Serer 14.7%, Diola 3.7%
Religions: Islam 94%, Christian 5%
Literacy Rate: 40 %
Currency: CFA Franc

Thailand

Capital: Bangkok
Area: 197,595 sq mi
Population: 67,400,750 (20th*)
Largest Cities: Bangkok 8,426,000
Life Expectancy: 73.8 yrs
Languages: Thai
Ethnicity: Thai 75%, Chinese 14%
Religions: Buddhists 94.6%, Muslim 4.8%
Literacy Rate: 96 %
Currency: Baht

* World ranking by population

Cue Cards   *Nations of the World*

Turkey

Capital: Ankara
Area: 297,591 sq mi
Population: 76,690,500 (18th*)
Largest Cities: Istanbul 11,253,000 Ankara 4,194,000, Izmir 2,927,000
Life Expectancy: 72.8 yrs
Languages: Turkish, Kurdish, Azeri
Ethnicity:: Turkish 70%, Kurdish 18%, Circassian 3%, Arab 1%
Religions: Muslim (Sunni) 99.8%. Others mostly Christian and Jews
Literacy Rate: 87.4%
Currency: Turkish Lira (YTL : yeni Turk lira)

Venezuela

Capital: Caracas
Area: 340,560 sq mi
Population: 31,292,700 (41st*)
Largest Cities: Caracas 5,243,300; Maracaibo 2,131,000; Valencia 1,866,000
Life Expectancy: 74.1 yrs
Languages: Spanish, numerous indigenous
Ethnicity: Spanish
Religions: Roman Catholic 96%
Literacy Rate: 93%.
Currency: Bolivar

Ukraine

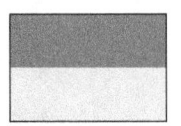

Capital: Kiev
Area: 233,089 sq mi
Population: 44,646,100 (31st*)
Largest Cities: Kiev 2,847,000, Kharkiv 1,441,000; Odessa 1,003,700
Life Expectancy: 68.74 yrs
Languages: Ukrainian 67%, Russian 24%,
Ethnicity: Ukrainian 77.8%, Russian 17.3%, Belorussiian
Religions: Ukrainian Orthodox 77%
Literacy Rate: 87.4%.
Currency: Ukrainian Hryvnia

Vietnam

Capital: Hanoi
Area: 125,622 sq mi
Population: 92,547,000 (14th*)
Largest Cities: Ho Chi Minh City 8,190,775; Hanoi 2,955,000; Haiphong 925,000
Life Expectancy: 72.4 yrs
Languages: Vietnamese, English, French
Ethnicity: Kinh (Viet) 86.2%, Tay 1.9%, Thai 1.7%, Muong 1.5%, Others
Religions: None 73%, Buddhist 12%, Catholic 7%, Hoa Hao 2%, Cao Dai 5%
Literacy Rate: 94%.
Currency: Dong

* World ranking by population

Cue Cards *Presidents of the United States*

George Washington (1732-1799)
Party: Federalist ★ Term: 1789-1797
Birthplace: Virginia

John Adams (1735-1826)
Party: Federalist ★ Term: 1797-1801
Birthplace: Massachusetts

Thomas Jefferson (1743-1826)
Party: Democratic-Republican
Term: 1801-1809
Birthplace: Virginia

Abraham Lincoln (1809-1865)
Party: Republican ★ Term: 1861-1865)
Birthplace: Kentucky

William McKinley (1843-1901)
Party: Republican ★ Term: 1897-1901
Birthplace: Ohio

Theodore Roosevelt (1858-1919)
Party: Republican ★ Term: 1901-1909
Birthplace: New York

Official Whitehouse Portraits

Cue Cards *Presidents of the United States*

William H. Taft (1857-1930)
Party: Republican ★ Term: 1909-1913
Birthplace: Ohio

Woodrow Wilson (1856-1924)
Party: Democratic ★ Term: 1913-1921
Birthplace: Virginia

Warren G. Harding (1865-1923)
Party: Republican ★ Term: 1921-1923
Birthplace: Ohio

Calvin Coolidge (1872-1933)
Party: Republican ★ Term: 1923-1929
Birthplace: Vermont

Herbert Hoover (1874-1964)
Party: Republican ★ Term: 1929-1933
Birthplace: Iowa

Franklin D. Roosevelt (1882-1945)
Party: Democratic ★ Term: 1933-1945
Birthplace: New York

Cue Cards *Presidents of the United States*

Harry S Truman (1884-1972)
Party: Democratic ★ Term: 1945-1953
Birthplace: Missouri

Dwight D. Eisenhower (1890-1969)
Party: Republican ★ Term: 1953-1961
Birthplace: Texas

John F. Kennedy (1917-1963)
Party: Democratic ★ Term: 1961-1963
Birthplace: Massachusetts

Lyndon B. Johnson (1908-1973)
Party: Democratic ★ Term: 1963-1969
Birthplace: Texas

Richard Nixon (1913-1994)
Party: Republican ★ Term: 1969-1974
Birthplace: California

Gerald Ford (1913-2006)
Party: Republican ★ Term: 1974-1977
Birthplace: Nebraska

Cue Cards *Presidents of the United States*

Jimmy Carter (1924-)
Party: Democratic ★ Term: 1977-1981
Birthplace: Georgia

Ronald Reagan (1911-2004)
Party: Republican ★ Term: 1981-1989
Birthplace: Illinois

George Bush (1924-)
Party: Republican ★ Term: 1989-1993
Birthplace: Massachusetts

Bill Clinton (1946-)
Party: Democrat ★ Term: 1993-2001
Birthplace: Arkansas

George W. Bush (1946-)
Party: Republican ★ Term: 2001-2009
Birthplace: Connecticut

Barack Obama (1961-)
Party: Democrat ★ Term: 2009-2017
Birthplace: Hawaii

Cue Cards — Real Estate Listings

RIVER FRONTAGE. Economical home in good condition just a mile from downtown. Features a covered patio, new combination oil/wood furnace, eat-in kitchen, 2 bedrooms, and a detached 1-car garage. Vinyl siding and a metal roof make the exterior nearly maintenance free. $98,000.

BEAUTIFUL MOUNTAIN VIEW HOME. Conveniently located just outside the village on 10 acres, this home offers 9 bedrooms, 4 full baths, and 2 kitchens. In recent years it has been a licensed group home, complete with sprinkler and fire alarm systems. $259,000.

OVER 55 PARK. Very well maintained home in "over 55" park. Great location within the park on a dead end road. The back yard has many perennials and trees. Screened porch offers total privacy. Park rent is $260 per month. $33,000.

WELL MAINTAINED HOME. Located in a private setting with landscaped stone walls & views of the White Mountains. Features a 3-car garage, woodstove, deck off the dining room as well as a guest room & kitchenette over the garage with private entrance. $235,000.

SPACIOUS HOME. Situated on 14+/- acres with beautiful pastoral views. It features large new windows, attached 2-car garage, outdoor oil or wood boiler, large barn and a brook running through the property. Your choice of local schools. $289,000.

COMPLETE PRIVACY. Timber frame home surrounded by 10 acres with beautiful White Mountain views. Built with 5 star energy rating. Features an open floor plan and a 2-car garage. Convenient to employment in VT and NH and offers choice of high school for your teens. $249,000.

Cue Cards *Real Estate Listings*

HOME WORTH LOOKING AT!
Lovely glassed-in entry porch, updated large oak cabineted kitchen w/new countertops. 2 BRs. Updates include vinyl siding, windows, metal roof, furnace, and electrical. Easy to maintain, good location. $87,500.

GEORGEOUS PRIVATE HOME
Sited on 10 acres. Built w/quality & lovingly maintained. covered porch overlooking a beautifully landscaped yard. 4BRs, 2½ baths, a finished, walk-out basement, and a 2-car attached garage. A must-see! $299,000.

COUNTRY FARMHOUSE
Lovely home sited on 2.5 acres on a "maple-tree-lined" country road. 4BRs, large open kitchen, formal dining room, double living room w/built-in bookshelves, new pellet stove/hearth, glassed-in porch, and side concrete patio. $199,000.

RECENTLY REDECORATED
Conveniently located in a pleasant residential neighborhood. Fireplaced living room, eat-in kitchen, den, 4BRs, a bath on each floor, plus a sunporch and an exercise room.. Attached 2-car garage, ample back yard, and large deck. $179,000.

ONE-ROOM SCHOOLHOUSE
Former schoolhouse in nearly original condition. Lg schoolhouse windows let in lots of light, chalkboard on the back wall, floor-to-ceiling bookcases. Used as a residential property for the past 20 yrs w/no real structural changes made. $69,500.

GORGEOUS 36 ACRES W/CAMP AND POND
Surveyed land w/a proposed subdivision. mostly wooded parcel w/one open field. Great potential for building a private home, or use the camp for hunting, snowmobiling, & 4-wheeling. Spectacular views from back corner. Lots of wildlife. $175,000.

Cue Cards — Real Estate Listings

ELEGANCE AND LUXURY PREVAIL
in this 4-bedroom, 3½ bath Colonial on 1.38 acres at Overlake View. Open floor plan, 9' ceilings, fireplaced family room, kitchen w/center island, master suite with tiled walk-in shower & jetted tub. Formal living & dining rooms. 5-car garage. Move-in ready. $820,000.

IN THE HEART OF THE TOWN
This charming 4-bedroom Colonial offers many updates, a fireplaced living room, applianced kitchen with granite countertops, formal living & dining room, and a brick hearth with woodstove in the family room. You are so close to everything. $429,000.

RESORT LIVING ALL YEAR LONG
Wonderful 3-level townhome ready for you to move right in & enjoy life on Lake Champlain at Marble Island. Quality features throughout, custom built-ins, fireplace, granite kitchen, balcony, lovely master suite, & fantastic views of the lake & mountains. $525,000.

8 ACRES WITH POND AND VIEW
Fish in the summer, skate in the winter, & entertain year round! Open plan with chef's kitchen with granite & floor to ceiling VT stone FP. Refinished hardwood floors, new carpet, freshly painted. Bonus room with gas stove, walkout basement with daylight windows, & more! $499,000.

A PLEASURE TO COME HOME TO!
You will feel at home the moment you enter this immaculate 4-bedroom Colonial located in Brennan Woods. Decorative columns, arched entryway, 9' ceilings, hardwood floors, and great open floor plan. 4 bedrooms, 2½ baths, family room plus a lovely custom back deck. $432,000.

CITY LIVING!
3 levels of living in this townhome located on Lake Street. Hardwood flooring, open floor plan, wood-burning fireplace, walls of glass, master suite & lower level den/bedroom with ¾ bath. Enjoy all the amenities of living downtown. Views! $699,000.

Sort 'n' Stack

Brief Description

The students separate 40 – 60 words into categories. The activity may focus on a phonological feature, such as the number of syllables in a word, the pronunciation of a past tense suffix, transitive and/or intransitive verbs, irregular verb families, parts of speech, etc.

Purpose

This activity is probably best done as a review. For example, it can be used to review specific features of the language where the words in question may fall into different categories, such as words that take negative prefixes (un-, in-, im-, a-, dis-). It can be used to introduce a linguistic feature, such as phrasal verb categories (transitive – separable and inseparable, and intransitive).

Preparation

Divide 5" x 7" index cards into 15 rectangles as below.

If you are copying and cutting up one of the pages in this book and you are making more than one game, it is a good idea to use colored paper to keep the sets separate. In other words, if you
need to make 5 games, use 5 different colored sheets of paper or different colored index cards. (They often come in packs of 4 different colors. Use rubber bands or large envelopes to keep the sets separate.)

Procedure

1. Describe the nature of the problem to the students. For example, *Today we're going to review regular and irregular verbs.*

2. Put the students into groups. Although this game can be done by individuals playing against each other, part of the value of the activity comes from the linguistic interaction that happens when students decide collectively on which words go in which stack. For that reason, three or four students working together will usually produce more differences of opinion, and hence more discussion. It also works better if everyone in each group is about the same proficiency level so that one strong student doesn't dominate the activity.

3. Give each group a stack of mixed cards and let them work together. At this point, do not interfere or coach. Tell them that when they have finished you will check their results.

4. As each group finishes, check their stacks. Alternatively, after everyone has finished, check the solution together.

Variations

1. Put a time limit on the activity. As a rule of thumb, a maximum of 5 seconds per card requires a quick decision. In more challenging games, 10 seconds per card allows for some discussion.

2. Make it competitive. Give one negative point for every wrong answer.

3. Do it as a circle activity. The students sit in a circle. Tell them the categories, for example regular and irregular verbs, and have them write these headings at the top of a sheet of paper as column headings. Give them each an equal number of cards and tell them to write each word under the correct column. After an appropriate period of time, say "pass," and they pass the cards to the student on their right. When the cards have made a complete circle, compare the results.

Suggestions
  1. Regular and irregular verbs
*2. Irregular verbs by past participle endings
     – d ending: *make > made*
     – t ending: *bring > brought*
     – (e)n ending: *bite > bitten*
    *3.   Phrasal verbs, separable and inseparable
*4. Transitive and intransitive verbs
*5. Verbs followed by infinitives, gerunds, or either
*6. Adjective – preposition collocations
  7. Derivational Endings
     – adjectives: *-ous, -ic, -ive, -al*
     – "doer" nouns: *-er, -or, -ar, -ist, -ian*
     – verbs: *-ate, -ify, -ize*
  8. Number of syllables
*9. Placement of stress (on which syllable)

* *See sample games on the following pages.*

Sort 'n' Stack, 1 Past Participles

The past participles of these words have three different ending sounds, /en/n/, /t/, and /d/. After making the cards, mix them up and have the students make three stacks according to the ending sounds. Some of the verbs in this list are uncommon. Therefore, to use the game with lower-level students, use only the verbs they may be familiar with and perhaps a few new ones.

/en/n/	/en/n/	/t/
BEAT	FLY	BEND
BITE	FREEZE	BRING
BLOW	HIDE	BUILD
BREAK	SEE	BUY
CHOOSE	SHAKE	CATCH
DRAW	SHOW	CREEP
DRIVE	THROW	DEAL
FALL	WEAVE	LEAVE

55

Sort 'n' Stack, 1 Past Participles

/t/	/d/	/d/
LEND	FLEE	SELL
LOSE	HEAR	SLIDE
MEAN	LAY	SPEED
SEND	LEAD	STAND
SWEEP	MAKE	TELL
THINK	PAY	UNDERSTAND
WEEP	READ	WIND
	SAY	

Sort 'n' Stack, 2 Transitive and Intransitive Verbs   Level: Moderate

After making the cards, mix them up and give them to the students. They should make three stacks: (1) transitive verbs, (2) intransitive verbs, and (3) transitive or intransitive.

transitive

ACCEPT	DESTROY	KILL
BEAT	ENJOY	KNOW
BRING	EXPECT	LIKE
BUILD	FIND	MAKE
BUY	GIVE	SAY
CARRY	HAVE	TAKE
CATCH	HEAR	TELL
CAUSE	HOLD	WEAR

Sort 'n' Stack, 2 Transitive and Intransitive Verbs
intransitive

AGREE	HAPPEN	REMAIN
APPEAR	LAUGH	RISE
ARRIVE	LIE	SIT
BELONG	LIStEN	SLEEP
CARE	LIVE	STAND
COME	LOOK	STEP
DREAM	MATTER	TALK
FALL	OCCUR	THINK
GO	RAIN	WAIT

Sort 'n' Stack, 2 Transitive and Intransitive Verbs
transitive or intransitive

BREAK	ESCAPE	REMEMBER
CHANGE	FAIL	RIDE
CONTINUE	FIGHT	RUN
COOK	FLY	SEE
DRAW	GROW	SING
DRINK	HURT	TEACH
DRIVE	KISS	TURN
EAT	PLAY	UNDERSTAND
ENTER	READ	WRITE

Sort 'n' Stack, 3 Separable and Inseparable Phrasal Verbs   Level: Moderate

After making the cards, mix them up and give them to the students. They should make three stacks: (1) transitive separable, (2) transitive inseparable, (3) intransitive.

transitive separable		transitive inseparable
BLOW OUT	PUT OFF *(POSTPONE)*	CALL ON
CALL UP	TAKE OFF *(REMOVE)*	GET ALONG WITH
DO OVER	TALK OVER	GET AROUND
FILL OUT	THROW AWAY	GET OVER
GIVE UP	USE UP	GET THROUGH
LEAVE OUT		GO OVER
LOOK UP		LOOK INTO
PICK OUT		LOOK LIKE

Sort 'n' Stack, 3 Separable and Inseparable Phrasal Verbs

transitive inseparable		intransitive
PICK ON	COME OUT *(BE PUBLISHED)*	GO AWAY
PUT UP WITH	COME OVER	MAKE OUT *(DO)*
RUN INTO	COME TO *(WAKE UP)*	PASS OUT *(FAINT)*
RUN OUT OF	COME UP *(ARISE)*	SHOW UP *(APPEAR)*
TAKE OVER	FALL APART	TURN UP *(APPEAR)*
	GET BY	TURN OUT *(CONCLUDE)*
	GET UP	

Sort 'n' Stack, 4 Verb-Infinitive/Gerund Combinations   Level: Moderate

After making the cards, mix them up and give them to the students. They should make three stacks: (1) verb + infinitive, (2) verb + gerund, (3) verb + gerund or infinitive.

verb + infinitive

ALLOW	FORCE	PERSUADE
APPEAR	HAPPEN	PROMISE
CONVINCE	HOPE	REFUSE
DECIDE	INVITE	REMIND
DEMAND	LEARN	TEACH
DECEIVE	OFFER	TELL
ENCOURAGE	ORDER	WAIT
FAIL	PERMIT	WARN

Sort 'n' Stack, 4 Verb-Infinitive/Gerund Combinations
verb + gerund

AVOID	DISLIKE	PRACTICE
COMPLETE	ENJOY	QUIT
DELAY	FINISH	RECOMMEND
DENY	KEEP	UNDERSTAND
DISCUSS	POSTPONE	

Sort 'n' Stack, 4 Verb-Infinitive/Gerund Combinations
verb + gerund or infinitive

BEGIN	LOVE	START*
CHOOSE	PLAN	STOP*
FORGET*	PREFER	TRY*
INTEND	REGRET*	
LIKE	REMEMBER*	

* = MEANING DIFFERENCE

Sort 'n' Stack, 5 Adjective-Preposition Collocations   Level: Difficult:

After making the cards, mix them up and give them to the students. They should make five stacks: (1) adjective + to, (2) adjective + of, (3) adjective + with, (4) adjective + at/in, (5) adjective + at/by.

adjective + to		adjective + of
ACCEPTABLE	MARRIED	CONSCIOUS
ACCUSTOMED	OPPOSED	FOND
DEDICATED	RESIGNED	FULL
ESSENTIAL	SIMILAR	GUILTY
HOSTILE	SUPERIOR	IN FAVOR
INDEBTED	AFRAID	PROUD
INFERIOR	AWARE	SURE
LOYAL	CAPABLE	TIRED

Sort 'n' Stack, 5 Adjective-Preposition Collocations

adjective + with	adjective + at	adjective + by/at
BLESSED	EXPERT	ALARMED
BORED	GOOD	AMAZED
COVERED	LUCKY	ANNOYED
DELIGHTED	QUICK	ASTONISHED
IMPRESSED	SLOW	CONFUSED
INVOLVED		EMBARRASSED
PLEASED		EMPLOYED
SATISFIED		PUZZLED
		SHOCKED

Sort 'n' Stack, 6 Primary Stress Placement   Level: Intermediate:

After making the cards, mix them up and give them to the students. They should make four stacks: (1) primary stress on first syllable, (2) primary stress on second syllable, (3) primary stress on third syllable, (4) primary stress on fourth or fifth syllable.

first syllable		second syllable
ACCIDENT	OPPOSITE	ACCEPT
EVERYWHERE	PARAGRAPH	ACROSS
HUNDRED	POPULAR	AGREEMENT
INTERNET	PRESIDENT	ALLOW
JANUARY	SINGULAR	ASSISTANCE
MAGAZINE	SUPERMARKET	COMPUTER
MEDICINE	UNDERWEAR	CORRECTION
MEMORY	VIOLENCE	EMPLOYER

67

Sort 'n' Stack, 6 Primary Stress Placement

Level: Intermediate:

second syllable		third syllable
IMPORTANT	AFTERNOON	NATIONALITY
INCLUDE	APPLICATION	OCCUPATION
LOCATION	AUTOMOBILE	RESERVATION
MUSICIAN	CONVERSATION	SATISFACTION
PREDICTION	IMMIGRATION	SYMPATHETIC
TRANSLATION	INDEPENDENT	SYSTEMATIC
VACATION	INSTITUTION	UNIVERSITY
VOCABULARY	INTRODUCTION	
	INVITATION	

Sort 'n' Stack, 6 Primary Stress Placement

Level: Intermediate:

fourth syllable		fifth syllable
ACCULTURATION	EXAMINATION	DECOMPOSABILITY
APPENDICITIS	IDEOLOGICAL	HISPANIC AMERICAN
BACTERIOLOGY	INTERCOLLEGIATE	INSUBORDINATION
BIODIVERSITY	ELECTROMAGNET	INTERCONTINENTAL
CLASSIFICATION	NATIONAL PARK	INTERGOVERNMENTAL
DEFORESTATION	PRONUNCIATION	PRESIDENTIAL CANDIDATE
ELECTRIC LIGHT	VIRTUAL IMAGE	RE-EVALUATION

Note: With the placement of stress on the third, fourth, or fifth syllables, there may be some dialect differences among native speakers.

Improvicards

Note

There are several types of improvisations and improvised conversations. For a comprehensive review of conversation cards (Role Play, Interview, Chain Story, Talks, Problems, Discussions) see Pro Lingua Associates' *Conversation Inspirations*. For improvisations, see Pro Lingua's *Improvisations*.

Description (This description focuses mainly on paired one-on-one activities.)

Two paired cards are the basis for this activity. Two students receive a pair of cards, and each student follows the brief instructions on one card. The information on the cards usually describes a problem, objective, or point of view that stimulates interacting, conversation, and problem-solving.

Purpose

To stimulate a conversation in which the students are working with a minimum of cues. They are forced to improvise with the language they already know to carry out the brief instructions on the card.

Preparation

For each one-on-one improvisation, prepare two cards so that each card presents just one side of a situation. You can build in some potential conflict that the students can play with. For example, one card might say, *It's 10 a.m. You are the ticket agent at the bus station. The schedule has changed. The only morning bus now leaves at 9:30.* The other card says, *You have come fifteen minutes early to catch the 10:00 bus. Now get your ticket.*

Procedure

Note: There are many different ways to use these Improvicards. One basic procedure is described below.

1. Pair the students up and give each pair a set of paired cards. Tell them they should not share the information on the card with their partner. After they have read their cards, ask if anyone needs help, and if so give it confidentially to the asker. Then explain the rest of the procedure.

2. Tell the students to interact and that one card says "You begin." Urge them to use their imaginations. It is best to set a time limit, and one minute should be sufficient, although depending on the group, it could go on for three or four minutes. If space permits, spread them out around the room. Circulate and listen, but don't interfere.

3. When the time is up or everyone has finished and they are back in their seats, ask each pair to tell the rest of the class what happened, pausing for questions and comments from the listeners.

4. Ask for a volunteer pair to perform their improvised conversation for the entire class. When they have finished, get reactions and questions. If the class is slow to react, prod them with questions such as:
   > *Where did this take place?*
   > *When?*
   > *Who was involved?*
   > *What did X want?*
   > *What would you do/say in this situation?*

5. Continue with more performances as time and interest allow. (optional) Take notes on pronunciation, lexical, or grammatical errors and point them out to the class.

6. If possible also note conversation strategies, such as opening, continuing, closing a conversation, paraphrasing, asking for repetition, clarification, active listening, echoing, etc.

Variations

1. Award an "Oscar" to the best performance (the students can vote on this).

2. Have two pairs exchange cards. Pair 1 performs; pair 2 (having already done that improvisation) listens and compares the performances. Then reverse. Pair 2 performs; pair 1 listens.

3. Do the activity completely impromptu. Call two students to the front; give them two cards. They read their cards to the class and then begin the improvisation as the class listens and watches.

4. Have the students create Improvisations.

Suggestions

1. Asking for help*

2. Shopping*
   food
   souvenirs
   clothing
   accessories
   specialty shop(s)
   used/new car

3. Transportation and travel
   bus
   taxi
   subway
   street directions
   air
   motel/hotel

4. Health and safety
   doctor
   dentist
   emergency room
   exercise club
   pharmacy

5. Housing
   roommate relationships
   apartment hunting
   repairs

6. Financial
   bank
   credit card
   personal loan

7. Education
   registration
   tests
   meeting a teacher

8. Services
   computer/phone/camera shop
   computer repair shop
   barber/beautician
   laundromat
   photo processing
   renting a car
   car repair
   service station
   post office
   police

9. Recreation/Entertainment
   cocktail party
   bar scene
   restaurant
   museum
   barbecue

See sample games on the following pages.

Improvicards   *Asking for Help 1*

1A

You are in a cafeteria. You can't find your dictionary.

YOU BEGIN

1B

It's lunchtime in the cafeteria. Your friend has lost their dictionary. Ask them to think where they have been this morning.

2A

The teacher asked you to make coffee for the class. You are not familiar with the coffeemaker. You see a student from another class. Ask for help.

YOU BEGIN

2B

A student from another class asks you how to use the coffee maker. Explain how.

3A

You are checking out City College campus. However, it's Sunday and the campus is very quiet. You are thirsty. You want to find a cold drink machine. Ask for help.

YOU BEGIN

3B

You are a student at City College. A stranger asks you for help. Give them directions or offer to take them. Find out who they are.

Improvicards *Asking for Help 2*

4A

You live in an apartment building. It's cold and you are not getting enough heat. You see the owner walking toward you.

YOU BEGIN

4B

You own an apartment building. The old heating system needs repairs that will cost a lot. It does produce heat, but you know it could be better. On the other hand, the rent for your apartments is quite low.

5A

You are on a commuter train. You have been sleeping. You wake up to discover the train has passed your stop. Ask the person beside you for help/advice.

YOU BEGIN

5B

You are on a commuter train going home. It has been a long hard day and you're tired. The person beside you has been sleeping for the last half-hour. They have just woken up and ask for your help.

6A

It's hot. You are walking down the street with a friend who isn't feeling well. Suddenly your friend collapses on the sidewalk. You are right in front of a shoe store. Go in and ask for help.

YOU BEGIN

6B

You are the owner of a shoe store. You have no help today and two people are trying on shoes. Suddenly someone rushes in and asks for help.

Improvicards

Asking for Help 3

7A

You twisted your ankle while walking in the park. You found a bench to sit on. Your ankle is very painful. It is 200 meters to the nearest street. Maybe you can get a taxi there. Ask someone to help you.

YOU BEGIN

7B

You are walking your dog through the park on the way home. Someone sitting on a bench asks you for help.

8A

You were hiking the Wilderness Trail on Wild Mountain and you took a wrong turn. You tried to take a short cut back to the Wilderness Trail, but now you're lost. Call 911.

YOU BEGIN

8B

You are the responder on 911. Someone calls to say they are lost. You could call for a rescue party, but you know the mountain very well.

9A

You think you left your small backpack at the restaurant where you had lunch. Go back and ask the host about it.

YOU BEGIN

9B

You are the host at a very busy restaurant. Someone comes to you with a problem. Respond.

Improvicards *Shopping 1*

1A

You read in the paper that Jaymart is having a big sale on TransCo laptops. The ad says "Special this Week." You decide to go to the Electronics department to buy one. Talk to a sales clerk.

YOU BEGIN

1B

You are a sales clerk at Jaymart. You are having a sale on TransCo laptops his week, but you just sold the last one. Yes, the ad says "Special this Week," but the fine print says "Limited Quantities; No rain checks."

2A

You are in the checkout line at JayMart, and you have picked up six small items to buy. The total is $27.45. You're about to pay, but you discover that you have only $20.00 and you left your credit cards at home.

2B

You are the checkout cashier at Jaymart. It's very busy. A customer has just purchased several small items. The total is $27.45.

YOU BEGIN

3A

You just bought a $10 magazine. You are sure you gave the clerk $50. You received $10 in change. Speak to the clerk about this.

YOU BEGIN

3B

You sell magazines, cigarettes, and candy all day long. You make change constantly. You think you are very accurate. A person just bought a $10 magazine with a $20 bill and you gave them $10.

Improvicards *Shopping 2*

4A Three days ago you bought a birthday gift for your mother – a nice winter sweater on sale for only $35.00. But it's really too large. So you got her something else. Take the sweater back to the store. *YOU BEGIN*	**4B** You own a small clothing store. You recently held a clearance sale and sold all your winter sweaters. The spring clothes have just arrived. You really don't want this winter sweater.
5A You are a university student. You don't have much money, but you'd like to have a car. You have $500 cash and a part-time job – $150 a week. You see a Kia that you like. It's $300 down and $350/month for 12 months.	**5B** You own a used car lot. Business is slow, and you'd like to sell something today. A customer seems interested in the Kia that you paid $3500 for last month. Approach the customer. *YOU BEGIN*
6A This morning you bought a new paperback novel ($9.95) by your favorite author. When you get home, you realize your spouse also bought a copy at the same store. Your spouse started to read it during lunch hour. Yours is still in a bag. Take it back to the store and explain. *YOU BEGIN*	**6B** You own a book store. The Internet and ebooks are hurting your business. A new novel has just come out and you've sold several in the past few days. That makes you feel better. A customer approaches.

Improvicards *Shopping 3*

7A

You like the display in a gift shop window, and you go inside for a look. You don't intend to buy anything, but you might if you see something very interesting. And anyway, you simply enjoy looking around and checking prices.

7B

You are the owner of a small gift shop. Recently you have lost some expensive gifts to shoplifters. A customer enters your shop and starts looking around, picking things up, and looking at prices. You are suspicious and nervous. Maybe it would be a good idea to get rid of this person because two more customers have just come in.

YOU BEGIN

8A

You see a very valuable antique clock in an antiques shop. You want it, but the price tag says $450. You have only $125 in cash and $350 in your checking account. You don't want to use your credit card. Make an offer.

YOU BEGIN

8B

You own an antiques shop. Business has been slow, and you do have some big bills to pay in the next few days. You don't like to bargain – you believe in fixed prices, but . . .

9A

You have just bought a small item in a gift shop that is full of fragile things in places where they could be knocked over. You hand the clerk your money, and at the same time your jacket sleeve knocks over a small figurine perched on top of the counter. CRASH!

9B

You own a gift shop with thousands of knickknacks. You never seem to have space enough for everything. You placed a small figurine ($18.75) on the counter by the cash register. A customer has just handed you some money and knocked over the figurine. It has broken.

YOU BEGIN

Correctocards

Brief Description

This is a quiz game. On each card there is a mistake and on the same side the correction. A player draws a card and reads the mistake to the opponent. The opponent attempts to answer and the card holder gives the correction. If the opponent is correct, they get one point or move up one step on one of the stairs on page 81.

Purpose

This is a review of lexical and/or grammatical points or subject matter that is either about general knowledge or part of the learner's course work, The sample cards were chosen to exemplify the great variety of language and content that students can work on – anything from history or civics to math or sciences.

Preparation

For each game prepare a set of 24 cards, each with a mistake and its correction on the same side of the card. Try to order the cards from easy to difficult.

Procedure

1. After selecting a topic and creating cards, place a stack of cards in front of the two opponents (two individuals or two teams) and give each of them a score card or the stairs on page 81.

2. Player/Team A takes the top card and reads the mistake to player/team B. If B answers correctly they move up one step using a coin or other marker. Then player/team B reads the next card and A tries to correct the mistake.

3. Play continues as each opponent climbs the stairs. The first to reach the top is the winner.

4. If neither player reaches the top, and all the cards have been used, the player with the most correct responses wins.

Variations

1. The game can be played with a non-playing quizmaster (or teacher) posing the questions to both teams. Any player from either team can say "BUZZ" for a chance to answer. The first player to buzz tries to answer. If the buzzer gives the wrong answer, the opponent gets a chance to answer. If no one buzzes, play continues to the next card. When all the cards have been used, the player with the most correct answers wins.

2. The teacher can read the entire class the incorrect sentence, and the students write their corrections. When all the cards are played, the correct answers are given and a winner is determined.

3. The stairs can have "lucky/unlucky" steps. Highlight a few steps; if a player lands on one of them, the player can gain or lose a step, according to the directions. The middle step where the stairs cross can be extra lucky/unlucky.

4. If one player reaches the top and there are still some cards to be played, The other player can be given a chance to catch up by answering the remaining cards.

Suggestions

1. Wrong word choice: "Can you borrow me five dollars?"*

2. Wrong word form: "My sister bringed me home."*

3. Wrong word order: "I picked up her at two o'clock."

4. Syntax mistake: "She no is my friend."*

5. Incorrect general facts: "There are fifteen planets."

6. Incorrect history facts: "Kennedy was assassinated in Chicago."

7. Incorrect science information: "Water boils at 100° Fahrenheit."

8. Incorrect local information: "The mayor of our town is (student's name)."

See sample games on the following pages.

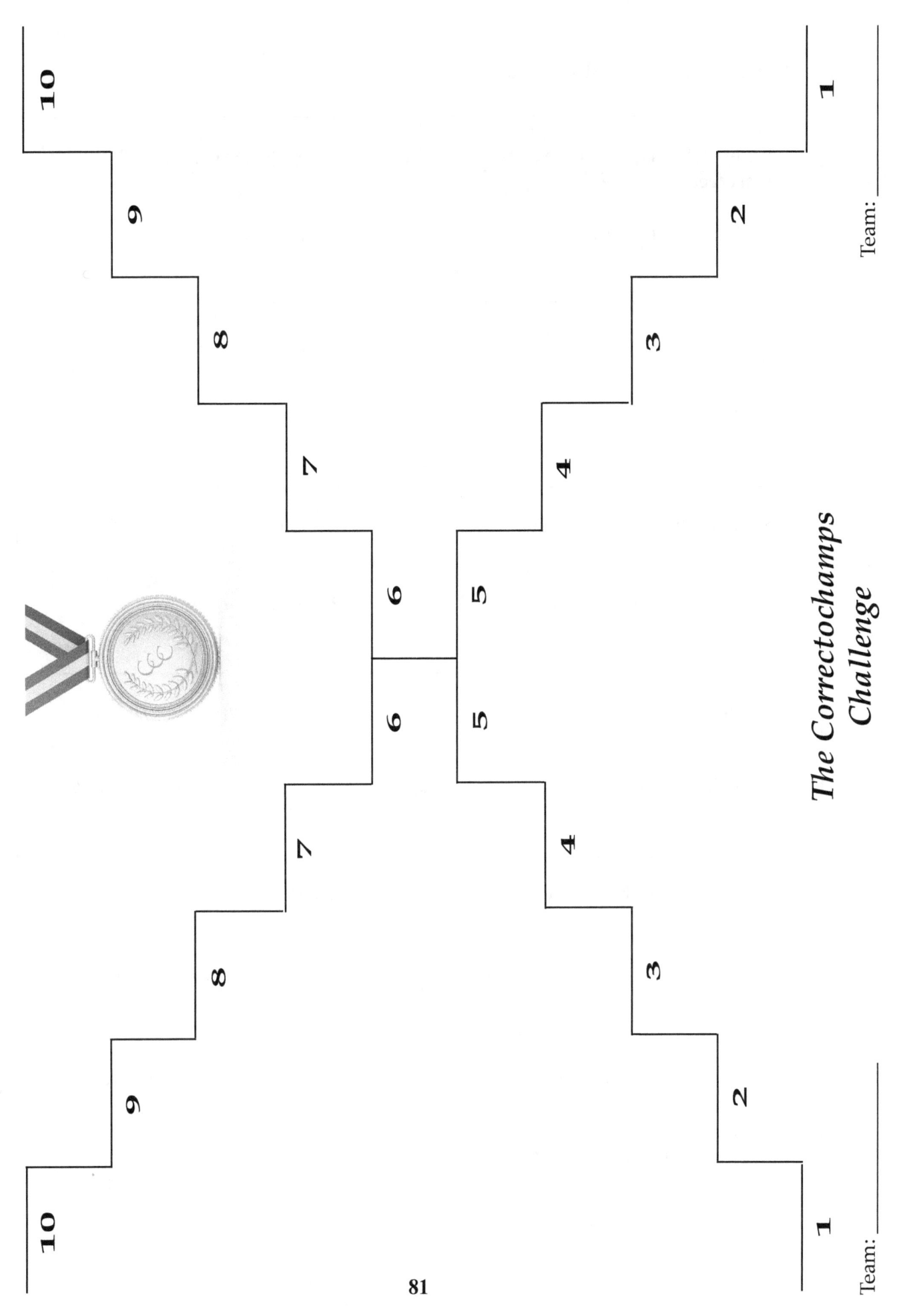

Correctocards 1, Word Choice

1. My brother is <u>too</u> tall. He's over six feet. *My brother is <u>very</u> tall.*	2. How <u>high</u> are you, six feet? *How <u>tall</u> are you, six feet?*
3. She <u>looked at</u> TV all night. *She <u>watched</u> TV all night.*	4. Will you <u>borrow</u> me your pen? *Will you <u>lend</u> me your pen?*
5. My mother works very <u>hardly</u>. *My mother works very <u>hard</u>.*	6. Did you <u>drink</u> all your soup? *Did you <u>eat</u> all your soup?*
7. I didn't <u>make</u> my homework. *I didn't <u>do</u> my homework.*	8. He can <u>talk</u> Japanese very well. *He can <u>speak</u> Japanese very well.*
9. She <u>performs</u> the piano very well. *She <u>plays</u> the piano very well.*	10. That is not a very <u>heavy</u> problem. *That is not a very <u>big</u> problem.*
11. Please <u>say</u> me the answer again. *Please <u>tell</u> me the answer again.*	12. It's time to get up and get <u>dressing</u>. *It's time to get up and get <u>dressed</u>.*

Correctocards 1, Continued

13. The traffic was very <u>heavily</u> today. *The traffic was very <u>heavy</u> today.*	14. Some of the stores are <u>giving</u> a sale. *Some of the stores are <u>having</u> a sale.*
15. That was a very <u>displeasant</u> moment. *That was a very <u>unpleasant</u> moment.*	16. The river <u>floated</u> the center of the town. *The river <u>flooded</u> the center of the town.*
17. I was very <u>irritating</u> by his behavior. *I was very <u>irritated</u> by his behavior.*	18. Yesterday I <u>did</u> fishing at Round Lake. *Yesterday I <u>went</u> fishing at Round Lake.*
19. It's so dark in here it's difficult to <u>look</u>. *It's so dark in here it's difficult to <u>see</u>.*	20. Yesterday I <u>dropped</u> down and hurt my knee. *Yesterday I <u>fell</u> down and hurt my knee.*
21. My brother is a <u>cooker</u> at the new restaurant. *My brother is a <u>cook</u> at the new restaurant.*	22. Can you tell me the <u>true</u> answer to this problem? *Can you tell me the <u>right/correct</u> answer to this problem?*
23. I <u>wish</u> I <u>can</u> go to Boston with you tomorrow. *I <u>hope</u> I can go to Boston with you tomorrow.* *I wish I <u>could</u> go to Boston with you tomorrow.*	24. If you do that, it will be the end of our <u>friendliness</u>. *If you do that, it will be the end of our <u>friendship</u>.*

Correctocards 2, Wrong Word Form

1. My sister <u>bringed</u> me home. *My sister <u>brought</u> me home.*	2. Somebody <u>stealed</u> my cell phone. *Somebody <u>stole</u> my cell phone.*
3. Where did I <u>left</u> it? *Where did I <u>leave</u> it?*	4. My new shirt <u>costed</u> a lot. *My new shirt <u>cost</u> a lot.*
5. I <u>seen</u> him yesterday afternoon. *I <u>saw</u> him yesterday afternoon.*	6. There were two <u>mens</u> in the room. *There were two <u>men</u> in the room.*
7. <u>He</u> is my sister. *<u>She</u> is my sister.*	8. Those are <u>hers</u> books. *Those are <u>her</u> books.*
9. This is mine; where is <u>your</u>? *This is mine; where is <u>yours</u>?*	10. I think she <u>prefer</u> the red one. *I think she <u>prefers</u> the red one.*
11. Does she <u>has</u> enough money? *Does she <u>have</u> enough money?*	12. She <u>haven't</u> done that before. *She <u>hasn't</u> done that before.*

Correctocards 2, Continued

13. Where is my keys? *Where are my keys?*	14. I have a fork and two knifes. *I have a fork and two knives.*
15. My sister is more taller than me. *My sister is taller than me.* *My sister is taller than I am.*	16. My grandmother moves very slow now. *My grandmother moves very slowly now.*
17. I'm sorry, your answer is uncorrect. *I'm sorry, your answer is incorrect.*	18. Mexico deports a lot of vegetables to the U.S. *Mexico exports a lot of vegetables to the U.S.*
19. When did the revolutionary begin? *When did the revolution begin?*	20. My brother doing very well at school. *My brother is doing very well at school.*
21. My friend Bob was baseball player. *My friend Bob was a baseball player.*	22. Were they many people in the room? *Were there many people in the room?*
23. The most biggest surprise was her success. *The biggest surprise was her success.*	24. Don't count your chicken before they hatch. *Don't count your chickens before they hatch.*

Correctocards 3, Grammar Problems

1. I no have enough money. *I don't/do not have enough money.*	2. My friend no is in class today. *My friend is not in class today.*
3. I don't have no money. *I don't have any money.*	4. She didn't bought anything. *She didn't buy anything.*
5. Where you going this weekend? *Where are you going this weekend?*	6. When you came to this city? *When did you come to this city?*
7. Does she has the right answer? *Does she have the right answer?*	8. My friends and I went yesterday downtown. *My friends and I went downtown yesterday.*
9. Who you gave the book to? *Who did you give the book to?* *To whom did you give the book?*	10. Is raining hard today. *It is raining hard today.*
11. Were twenty people on the bus. *There were twenty people on the bus.*	12. That my book on the teacher's desk. *That is my book on the teacher's*

Correctocards 3, Continued

13. I am not understanding what you said. *I don't understand what you said.*	14. Who is knowing the answer? *Who knows the answer?*
15. Please give to me that package. *Please give me that package.* *Please give that package to me.*	16. I will pick up her at five o' clock. *I will pick her up at five o'clock.*
17. Never she makes that mistake. *She never makes that mistake.*	18. I buy always my clothes at Spencer's. *I always buy my clothes at Spencers.*
19. I am going to go tomorrow there. *I am going to go there tomorrow.*	20. I am not able going there tomorrow. *I am not able to go there tomorrow.*
21. We gotta go now. *We have got to go now.* *We've got to go now.*	22. I ate too much apples. *I ate too many apples.*
23. I don't know where does she live. *I don't know where she lives.*	24. Do you plan driving to Omaha? *Do you plan to drive to Omaha?* *Do you plan on driving to Omaha?*

Correctocards 4, World Geography

1. The French Channel separates France and England. *The <u>English</u> Channel separates France and England.*	2. The Bavarian Alps are in Switzerland. *The Bavarian Alps are in <u>Germany</u>.*
3. Portugal shares a border with Italy. *Portugal shares a border with <u>Spain</u>.*	4. The capital of Spain is Barcelona. *The capital of Spain is <u>Madrid</u>.*
5. The Vatican City is in Paris. *Vatican City is in <u>Rome</u>.*	6. Istanbul is in Asia. *Istanbul is in <u>Asia and Europe</u>.*
7. The Adriatic Sea is between Greece and Turkey. *The <u>Aegean</u> Sea is between Greece and Turkey.* *The Adriatic Sea is between Italy and Greece, Albania, Serbia, and Croatia.*	8. Alexandria is the largest city in Egypt. *<u>Cairo</u> is the largest city in Egypt.*
9. The capital of Iran is Mashad. *The capital of Iran is <u>Teheran</u>.*	10. Thailand was once called Burma. *Thailand was once called <u>Siam</u>.* *<u>Myanmar</u> was once called Burma.*
11. Kangaroos are found in the Philippines. *Kangaroos are found in <u>Australia</u>.*	12. The capital of Pakistan is Karachi. *The capital of Pakistan is <u>Islamabad</u>.*

Correctocards 4, Continued

13. Kazakhstan has a 500-mile ocean coastline. *Kazakhstan has <u>no</u> ocean coastline.*	14. Ho Chi Minh City used to be called Hanoi. *Ho Chi Minh City used to be called <u>Saigon</u>.*
15. New Zealand is northeast of Australia. *New Zealand is <u>southeast</u> of Australia.*	16. Farsi is the national language of Uzbekistan. *Farsi is the national language of <u>Iran</u>.* *<u>Uzbeki</u> is the national language of Uzbekistan.*
17. Budapest is on the Rhine River. *Budapest is on the <u>Danube</u> River.*	18. The Atlantic Ocean is the largest ocean in the world. *The <u>Pacific</u> Ocean is the largest ocean in the world.*
19. Somalia is north and east of Ethiopia. *Somalia is <u>south</u> and east of Ethiopia.*	20. Mount Kilimanjaro is in Mozambique. *Mount Kilimanjaro is in <u>Tanzania</u>.*
21. The most populous country in Africa is Sudan. *The most populous country in Africa is <u>Nigeria</u>.*	22. The lingua franca of Angola is French. *The lingua franca of Angola is <u>Portuguese</u>.*
23. Tagalog is spoken in Malaysia. *Tagalog is spoken in <u>the Philippines.</u>*	24. Hokkaido is Japan's largest island. *<u>Honshu</u> is Japan's largest island.*

Quiz Cards

Brief Description

This is a simple quiz game, similar to Correctocards. There is a question and its answer on each card. One team or person asks a question and another answers it. The game can be played as a race to a goal. See the "Ladders" on page 93.

Purpose

To practice listening and speaking skills as well as the grammatical structure of questions. The game can also be exciting because of the competitive aspect, but it achieves its purpose only if the students are conversing together in English as they formulate answers to the questions. In other words, be very strict about the use of the students' native language.

Preparation

The questions you choose can be from virtually any content area. As you prepare a game, it is preferable to focus on one content area, such as "sports." The Internet and dictionaries are good sources for questions. Also consider your students' backgrounds as you choose the topic and questions.

There are three types of questions that work well with this game:

1. **Information questions** (Usually a question word such as *what, who,* and *where* begins the question.)
2. **True-False questions**, which require only a one-word answer.
3. **Multiple Choice questions,** which require close listening to a list of three possible answers (a four-item multiple choice is a bit challenging for an aural multiple choice).

As you prepare the game it is advisable, after you have selected the topic, to use only one type of question form for each game – for example, True/False questions. It is also useful to try to have all the questions and answers at the same proficiency level.

The ladders on page 93 are optional, but they can add a visual aspect to the competition.

Procedure

1. Describe the nature of the game to the students. Also be sure they understand the type of question that will be used in the game.

2. Divide the class into teams of 3 or 4 team members each. Give each team a name. For fun, use animal names that are alliterative with one team member's name – for example, Antonio's Antelopes, Keiko's Kangaroos, Mehmet's Marmots.

3. One person on Team A draws a card and asks Team B the question. Team B has 30 seconds to discuss and answer it (a desktop bell would be useful). A spokesperson gives the team's answer, and the asker confirms if it is right or wrong. Award one point for a correct answer, and one step on the ladder.

4. If there are more than two teams, the asking and answering proceeds serially. If there are four teams, it goes like this: A asks B, B asks C, C asks D, D asks A, etc. Be sure each team has the same number of answering opportunities, and try to be sure that the asking and answering roles are rotated on each team.

Variations

1. You can ask the questions. With this type of arrangement, you can allow one team to answer, and a second or third team to challenge. Award double points for a successful challenge, and a negative point for an unsuccessful one.

2. With three teams, one asks, the second answers, and the third either agrees or disagrees. For scoring, successful answers and confirmation receive a point (or take a step) and an unsuccessful response loses a point/step.

3. You could establish different types of questions on each topic:
    1 point for True-False questions
    2 points for Multiple Choice questions
    3 points for Information questions

    The students can choose the type of question they want. Alternatively, be sure each team gets an equal number of each type.

4. If you have several topics, let the students choose the topic.

5. You ask the questions. Give each team a "buzzer" and let the first to "buzz" try to answer. This works best if negative points are assigned to incorrect answers, and the other team(s) gets a chance to try or decline the questions.

Note: *See page 176 for the Pro Lingua Phonetic Alphabet used with these cards.*

1. Country facts
2. Famous people* True-False questions
3. Geographical features (mountains, lakes, deserts, waterfalls)
4. International sports and Olympics
5. Historical facts
6. Animals
7. Languages
8. Word definitions* Multiple Choice questions
9. Engineering achievements (buildings, dams, bridges, tunnels)
10. Word spellings*
11. Films
12. Music
13. Books
14. Health and nutrition
15. Weather and climate
16. Inventions
17. Astronomy* Information questions

See sample games on the following pages.

The following games are available in *Index Card Games for ESL*.

    Measurement
    U.S. Facts
    World Facts
    Dynamic Duos (Pair Collocations)
    Idioms
    Proverbs
    U.S. History
    Academy Awards (Best Picture)
    Currencies
    Abbreviations and Acronyms

Quiz Cards Game 1, Famous People — *True or False?*

1. Cleopatra was married to Julius Caesar at one time. ***FALSE.*** She was his lover. She married Mark Antony.	2. Copernicus was a Polish astronomer and mathematician. ***TRUE.***
3. Columbus died shortly after his second voyage to the New World. ***FALSE.*** He died two years after his fourth voyage.	4. The Portuguese explorer Magellan attempted to sail around the world, but he died en route in the Philippines. ***TRUE.*** He died in the Battle of Mactan in the Philippines in 1521.
5. William Shakespeare wrote plays and short stories. ***FALSE.*** He wrote plays and poems.	6. Queen Elizabeth the First never married. ***TRUE.***
7. Napoleon was more than six feet tall. ***FALSE.*** He was 5'6".	8. Benito Juárez was the first Indian (Zapotec) president of Mexico. ***TRUE.*** He was President from 1861 to 1872.

Quiz Cards Game 1, Famous People *True or False?*

9. George Washington owned African American slaves. ***TRUE.*** At the time of his death he owned over 100 slaves. In his will he gave them their freedom.	10. Ludwig Van Beethoven was born in Vienna. ***FALSE.*** He was born in Bonn, Germany.
11. Alfred Nobel invented dynamite. ***TRUE.*** Later he created the famous prizes.	12. The *Mona Lisa* was painted by Leonardo da Vinci. ***TRUE.***
13. Mark Twain's most famous book was *Moby Dick*. ***FALSE.*** *Huckleberry Finn* was his most famous book. Herman Melville wrote *Moby Dick*.	14. President Theodore Roosevelt was President Franklin Roosevelt's father. ***FALSE.*** They were fifth cousins.
15. Babe Ruth was a great football player. ***FALSE.*** He was a great baseball player.	16. Ernest Hemingway wrote "For Whom the Bell Tolls." ***TRUE.***

Quiz Cards Game 1, Famous People　　　　　　　　　　　　*True or False?*

17. Atatürk was the president of Turkey during World War II. *FALSE.* He died before World War II.	18. Winston Churchill was a British general during World War II. *FALSE.* He was the Prime Minister during World War II.
19. President Eisenhower ordered the dropping of the atomic bomb on Japan. *FALSE.* President Harry Truman gave the order.	20. Jackie Robinson was the first African-American to play professional basketball. *FALSE.* He was the first African American to play in American Major League Baseball.
21. Marilyn Monroe was married to a famous baseball player. *TRUE.* His name was Joe Dimaggio.	22. An Israeli and an Egyptian have shared the Nobel Peace Prize. *TRUE.* Menachim Begin and Anwar Sadat won the prize in 1978.
23. The great football (soccer) player Pele was from Argentina. *FALSE.* He was Brazilian.	24. President Richard Nixon was assassinated. *FALSE.* He resigned from office.

Quiz Cards Game 2, Word Definitions – Verbs
Multiple Choice Questions

To pacify PA Suh FAY 1. To make something or someone quiet. 2. To establish an agreement or contract. 3. To speak quietly. *Answer:* 1	**To parade** Puh RAID 1. To imitate or copy. 2. To attack in a military formation. 3. To walk or display in a public way. *Answer:* 3
To paralyze PAR uh LAYZ 1. To cause someone or something to be unable to move. 2. To go along beside the main idea. 3. To cause a chemical reaction. *Answer:* 1	**To paraphrase** PAR uh FRAIZ 1. To speak clearly. 2. To express a thought in another way. 3. To divide a long text into smaller sections. *Answer:* 2
To parrot PAR uhT 1. To dress in bright colors. 2. To repeat or imitate without understanding. 3. To push something to the side. *Answer:* 2	**To propose** PRuh POZ 1. To make a suggestion or offer. 2. To delay something for later. 3. To place something in front. *Answer:* 1
To poke POK 1. To put something in one's pocket. 2. To laugh at someone. 3. To push or prod, with a stick or finger. *Answer:* 3	**To plunge** PLUHNJ 1. To dive or jump quickly into something. 2. To investigate carefully. 3. To fill up a hole or container. *Answer:* 1

Quiz Cards Game 2, Word Definitions – Verbs
Multiple Choice Questions

To pierce PEERS 1. To drive a sharp object completely through something. 2. To gather things together. 3. To throw something violently. *Answer:* 1	**To plead** PLEED 1. To fold. 2. To beg. 3. To place firmly. *Answer:* 2
To preserve PRI **ZerV** 1. To save. 2. To finish work early. 3. To prepare. *Answer:* 1	**To proclaim** PRO **KLEYM** 1. To reserve in advance. 2. To insist vigorously. 3. To announce formally or officially. *Answer:* 3
To peddle PED uhL (P E D D L E) 1. To ride a bicycle. 2. To go from place to place selling things. 3. To interfere in someone else's business. *Answer:* 2 *Note:* Also spell the word.	**To penetrate** PEN uh TRAIT 1. To enter in a sharp way. 2. To write a very skillful analysis. 3. To send someone to prison. *Answer:* 1
To perish PER ISH 1. To remove the outer part. 2. To clean up. 3. To die. *Answer:* 3	**To persecute** Per Suh KYOOT 1. To accuse. 2. To oppress. 3. To flow. *Answer:* 2

Quiz Cards Game 2, Word Definitions – Verbs *Multiple Choice Questions*

To persuade Per **SWAID**

1. To argue with.
2. To agree with.
3. To convince.

Answer: 3

To pretend PRI **TEND**

1. To do something falsely.
2. To stretch.
3. To take care of.

Answer: 1

To perceive Per **SEEV**

1. To go forward.
2. To see; understand.
3. To become completely covered.

Answer: 2

To pursue Per **SOO**

1. To bring someone to court for a trial.
2. To read very carefully.
3. To follow someone.

Answer: 3

To purify **PYOOR** uh **FAY**

1. To cause something to have high religious status.
2. To make something completely empty.
3. To make something clean or free of other things.

Answer: 3

To publish **PUHB** LISH

1. To make something become very popular.
2. To tell the truth.
3. To produce a book.

Answer: 3

To provide PRuh **VAYD**

1. To see.
2. To make better.
3. To supply.

Answer: 3

To pause **PAWZ**

1. To think about something.
2. To stop briefly.
3. To state an idea or opinion.

Answer: 2

Quiz Cards Game 3, Spelling Bee *Easy*

ACHES /AIKS/ My head aches. AI - SEE - AICH - EE - ES	**ADVICE** /AD **VAYS**/ Let me give you some advice. AI - DEE - VEE - AY - SEE - EE
AFFECT /uh **FEKT**/ How did that affect you? AI - EF - EF - EE - SEE - TEE	**ALL RIGHT** /**AWL** **RAYT**/ Are you all right? AI - EL - EL AR - AY - JEE - AICH - TEE
ANSWER /**AN** Ser/ Please answer the question. AI - EN - ES - DUHBuhLYOO - EE - AR	**BEAUTIFUL** /**BYOO** TI FUL/ That picture is beautiful. BEE - EE - AI - YOO - TEE - AY - EF - YOO - EL
BELIEVE /Buh **LEEV**/ I don't believe you. BEE - EE - EL - AY - EE - VEE - EE	**CERTAIN** /**Ser** TIN/ I am not certain about that. SEE - EE - AR - TEE - AI - AY - EN

100

Quiz Cards Game 3, Spelling Bee *Easy*

CLOTHES /**KLOZ**/ You always wear beautiful clothes. SEE - EL - O - TEE - AICH - EE - ES	**COUGH** /**KAWF**/ Please cover your mouth when you cough. SEE - O - YOO - JEE - AICH
DOUBT /**DOUT**/ I doubt that she will agree with you. DEE - O - YOO - BEE - TEE	**EIGHT** /**AIT**/ Is it eight o'clock already? EE - AY - JEE - AICH - TEE
FEBRUARY /**FEB** YOO ER EE/ Lincoln's birthday is in February. EF - EE - BEE - AR - YOO - AI - AR - WAY	**FOREIGN** /**FOR** IN/ Are you a foreign student? EF - O - AR - EE - AY - JEE - EN
NIECE /**NEES**/ My brother's daughter is my niece. EN - AY - EE - SEE - EE	**PHYSICAL** /**FIZ** uh KuhL/ She is a physical education teacher. PEE - AICH - WAY - ES - AY - SEE - AI - EL

Quiz Cards Game 3, Spelling Bee   *Easy*

PRINCIPAL /**PRIN** Suh PuhL/ He is an elementary school principal. PEE - AR - AY - EN - SEE - AY - PEE - AI - EL	**QUITE** /KWAYT/ It's really quite easy to do that. KYOO - YOO - AY - TEE - EE
RECEIPT /RI **SEET**/ May I have a receipt, please? AR - EE - SEE - EE - AY - PEE - TEE	**SERIOUS** /**SEER** EE uhS/ She is a very serious student. ES - EE - AR - AY - O - YOO - ES
SPECIAL /**SPESH** uhL/ Today is a special day. Your birthday! ES - PEE - EE - SEE - AY - AI - EL	**STRAIGHT** /STRAIT/ Can you draw a straight line? ES - TEE - AR - AI - AY - JEE - AICH - TEE
SURE /SHOOR/ Are you sure about that? ES - YOO - AR - EE	**TIME** /TAYM/ What time is it? TEE - AY - EM - EE

Quiz Cards Game 4, Spelling Bee

Harder

ABSENCE   /AB SuhNS/
You can't have another absence; you've already missed three classes.

AI - BEE - ES - EE - EN - SEE - EE

ACHIEVE   /uh CHEEV/
Did you achieve all your goals?

AI - SEE - AICH - AY - EE - VEE - EE

EFFECT   /uh FEKT/
What effect did his decision have on your plans?

EE - EF - EF - EE - SEE - TEE

EXPECT   /EK SPEKT/
I expect you to be here tomorrow.

EE - EKS - PEE - EE - SEE - TEE

AISLE   /AYL/
The cat food is in aisle ten.

AI - AY - ES - EL - EE

APPRECIATE   /uh PREE SHEE AIT/
I really appreciate your assistance with this.

AI - PEE - PEE - AR - EE - SEE - AY - AI - TEE - EE

ARGUMENT   /AR GYOO MuhNT/
I think I lost the argument.

AI - AR - JEE - YOO - EM - EE - EN - TEE

BENEFICIAL   /BEN uh FISH uhL/
What we are proposing will be very beneficial; it will help a lot.

BEE - EE - EN - EE - EF - AY - SEE - AY - AI - EL

Quiz Cards Game 4, Spelling Bee *Harder*

CEMETERY /**SEM** uh TER EE/ My grandfather is buried in this cemetery. SEE - EE - EM - EE - TEE - EE - AR - WAY	**CONSCIOUS** /**KAHN** SHuhS/ The patient is conscious; she can hear you. SEE - O - EN - ES - SEE - AY - O - YOO - ES
DESSERT /Duh **ZerT**/ Will you have some cake for dessert? DEE - EE - ES - ES - EE - AR - TEE	**EFFICIENT** /uh **FISH** uhNT/ This new machine is very efficient; It will save you money and time. EE - EF - EF - AY - SEE - AY - EE - EN - TEE
RHYTHM /**RI** THuhM/ The rhythm in this poem is mostly da DA dada DA. AR - AICH - WAY - TEE - AICH - EM	**GUILTY** /**GIL** TEE/ The defendant was found guilty. JEE - YOO - AY - EL - TEE - WAY
HEIGHT / **HAYT**/ His height is at least six feet. AICH - EE - AY - JEE - AICH - TEE	**JEALOUS** /**JEL** uhS/ She was very jealous of his success. JAI - EE - AI - EL - O - YOU - ES

104

Quiz Cards Game 4, Spelling Bee *Harder*

LIGHTNING /**LAYT** NING/ During the storm the barn was hit by lightning. EL - AY - JEE - AICH - TEE - EN - AY - EN - JEE	**MAINTENANCE** /**MAIN** Tuh NuhNS/ My car requires very little maintenance; it's very reliable. EM - AI - AY - EN - TEE - EE - EN - AI - EN - SEE - EE
MISCELLANEOUS /MIS uh **LAI** NEE uhS/ The box was full of miscellaneous stuff. EM - AY - ES - SEE - EE - EL - EL - AI - EN - EE - O - YOO - ES	**MISSPELL** /MIS **SPEL**/ I always misspell this word. EM - AY - ES - ES - PEE - EE - EL - EL
PARALLEL /**PAR** uh LEL/ Parallel lines never meet. PEE - AI - AR - AI - EL - EL - EE - EL	**SCHEDULE** /**SKED** JOOL/ Do you have a bus schedule for Chicago? ES - SEE - AICH - EE - DEE - YOO - EL - EE
SEIZE /SEEZ/ "Seize the day" is a well-known saying. ES - EE - AY - ZEE - EE	**STATIONARY** /**STAI** SHuhN ER EE/ I can't move it; it is stationary. ES - TEE - AI - TEE - AY - O - EN - AI - AR - WAY

Quiz Cards Game 5, U.S. Geography

1. In what state is the Hudson River? New York	2. How many states are there in New England? Six: Maine, New Hampshire, Vermont, Massachusetts, Rhode Island, Connecticut
3. How many states have "North" or "South" in their names? Four: North and South Dakota and Carolina	4. One state has "West" in its name. What is its second name? Virginia
5. Which city is not in the United States: Buffalo, Minneapolis, or Calgary? Calgary. It's in Alberta, Canada.	6. What is the largest city in Florida in population? Jacksonville: 821,784 (2014 estimate)
7. Which is longer, the Missouri River or the Mississippi? The Missouri	8. How many lakes are there in the Great Lakes? Five

Quiz Cards Game 5, U.S. Geography

9. Name three of the Great Lakes. Superior, Michigan, Huron, Erie, Ontario	10. What state has the largest area? Alaska. 663,300 square miles (1.718 million km²)
11. Which state was the 50th state admitted to the union? Hawaii	12. In which state is The Grand Canyon? Arizona
13. How many states border on Mexico? Four: California, Arizona, New Mexico, Texas	14. How many states border on Canada? Eleven: ME, NH, VT, NY, MI, MN, ND, MT, ID, WA, AK
15. Key West is part of which state? Florida	16. Las Vegas is in which state? Nevada

Quiz Cards Game 5, U.S. Geography

17. What is the District of Columbia? The federal territory that includes Washington (D.C.)	18. Name three states that have a coastline on the Gulf of Mexico. Florida, Alabama, Mississippi, Louisiana, Texas
19. What is the largest city in California in population? Los Angeles: City – 3,884,307; Metro – 13,131,431 (2014 est.)	20. In what state is The Great Salt Lake? Utah
21. What is the smallest state in area? Rhode Island: 2,707 square miles	22. Which state is not on the Atlantic Ocean? Georgia? New Jersey? Kentucky? Kentucky
23. Boston is the capital of which state? Massachusetts	24. What state is just south of Washington state? Oregon

Mime Cards

Brief Description

A student has a card with words or phrases on it and, by using gestures and other conventions, mimes the meaning as other students guess what is on the card. This is similar to the party game "Charades" or "Silent Movie."

Purpose

To entertain, to create some conversation among the guessers, and stimulate the mimer's creativity at playing with language using antonyms, synonyms, homonyms, visual paraphrasing, and circumlocutions. The game can be a good warm-up or pace-breaker.

Preparation

There are three basic types of cards (see **Suggestions**). One type simply has a list of words that have some grammatical or lexical unity. Usually five or six words are sufficient for each card, although for students at lower proficiency levels with limited vocabulary, three words may be enough.

As you prepare the cards, keep in mind not only the students' proficiency level, but the nature of the word itself – is it easily mimed? The more abstract the word, the more difficult it will be. For example, "run" would be very easy – perhaps too easy; "believe" would be difficult.

The second type of card has idiomatic phrases such as comparative expressions with animals (*sly as a fox*). Since a phrase can sometimes be guessed almost immediately, the card should have at least two, but generally no more than four phrases. It is best to build sets that have some commonality – for example, semantic field (topic), or collocations.

The third type, similar to the party game, often involves longer phrases or sentences, such as a proverb (*Don't count your chickens before they hatch*), so that one phrase/sentence per card is sufficient. This type has to be carefully thought out, because what is common knowledge in Anglophone culture may be completely unknown to students from other cultures.

The game is usually more exciting if there is a competitive element, so that one or more teams of students are competing against each other.

Procedure

1. Explain the nature and purpose of the game to the students. At this point, you should establish time limits and some ground rules:
    – no sounds from the mimer
    – no pointing at or showing an object if the object is the word (If the word in question is *money*, the mimer cannot take money from their pocket and show it.)

2. Before beginning the game, it is necessary to establish some conventions, such as:

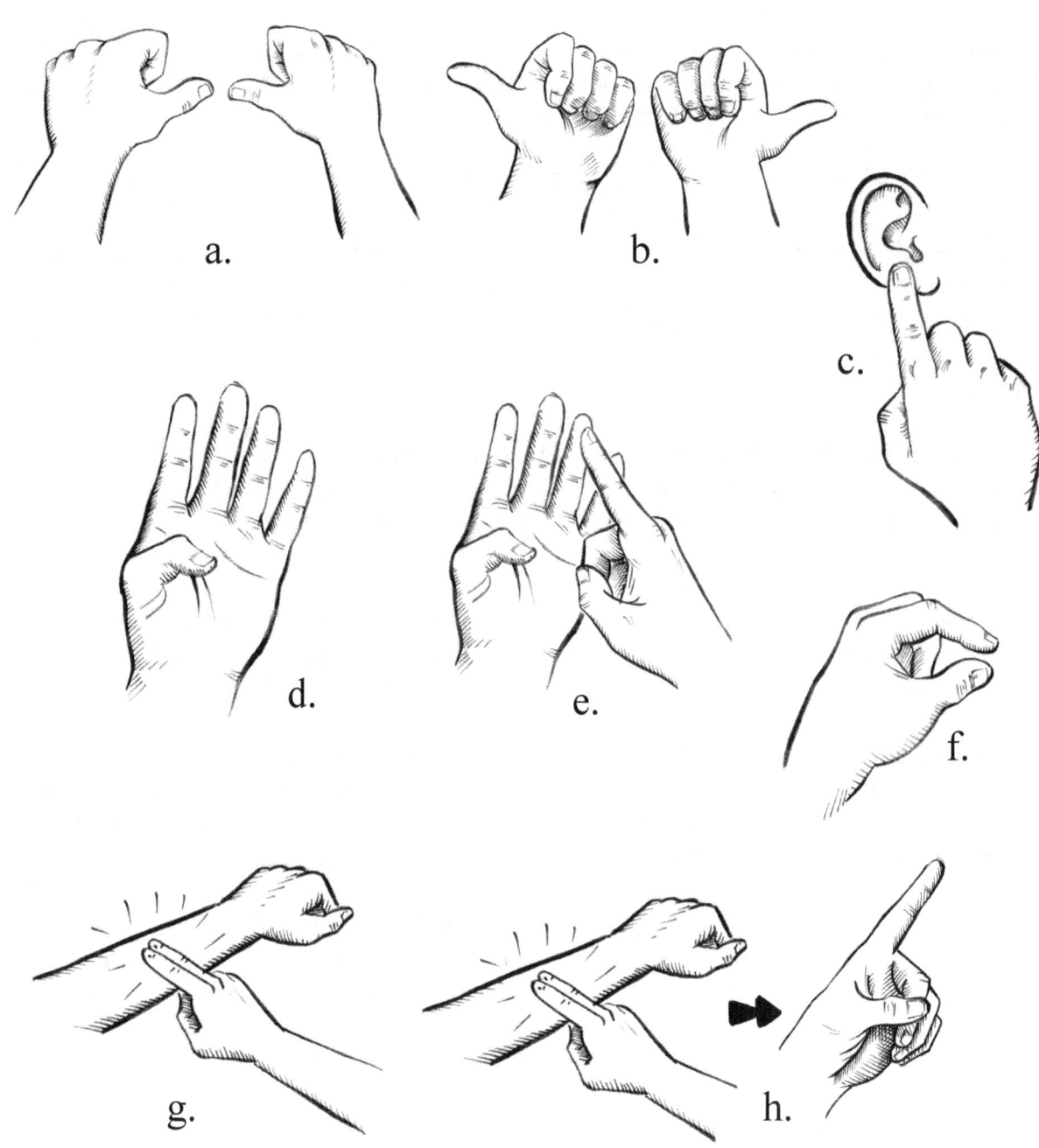

- a. synonym: thumbs and fists pointing to each other
- b. antonym: thumbs and fists going away from each other
- c. sounds like: finger to ear
- d. number of words (in a phrase/sentence): show fingers
- e. which word (immediately after number of words): show finger, e.g. third finger
- f. little words : thumb and index finger close together
- g. number of syllables: tap forearm
- h. which syllable (immediately after tappng forearm); show finger

3. Announce the type and category of the cards. For example, "Word List; five verbs." Incidentally, with a verb list, you could require the students to also give the three principal parts of the verb: for example: *go, went, gone*.

4. For a non-competitive game, divide the class into groups (four per group is a good group size). Give a student in one group a card. Show the other groups what is on the card so they can be passively involved as the game progresses. If the student doesn't understand something on the card, you can step outside with the student to explain it, or give the student another card.

5. Establish a time limit. The student mime should begin by showing how many words (with fingers), and then which word (finger). The student begins miming and the other students in the group begin calling out their guesses, until the mimer gives a "thumbs up."

6. Another group begins with a new word or phrase.

Variations

1. For a more competitive game, divide the class into groups of four students per group. Select a student from one of the groups to be the mime. When the mime begins, the groups take turns guessing the answer, one guess at a time, until one group gets the answer and a point.

2. The students can create their own cards. This usually has one advantage over prepared cards; the cards they produce should reflect the students' actual proficiency and knowledge.

Suggestions

1. Word list
   a. action verbs
   b. adjectives
   c. lexical sets such as nouns for transportation, sports, food.
   *d. compound words; for example: *brainstorm, hummingbird, fireplace*.

2. Short phrases
   *a. idioms such as *by heart, (to cost) an arm and a leg, a stick in the mud*
   b. comparative expressions: *busy as a beaver, harder than a rock*
   c. partitive expressions: *deck of cards, loaf of bread*
   d. collocations: *take a shower, do the dishes, make the bed*
   e. movie/book/song titles

3. Longer phrases and sentences
   *a. proverbs: *A bird in the hand is worth two in the bush.*
   b. sayings: *penny wise, pound foolish*

* *See sample games on the following pages.*

Mime Card Game 1, Compound Nouns *Easy*

basketball scorekeeper home run field goal	thunderstorm sunshine rainbow starlight	bathtub bookcase coffee table table lamp
tee shirt overcoat necktie underwear	pocketbook billfold lipstick key chain	bulldog horseshoe mountain lion catfish
police officer mail carrier city manager emergency medical technician	pencil sharpener paper clip photocopier letter opener	notebook ballpoint pen wastebasket white board
midnight moonlight daybreak afternoon	earthquake windstorm snowstorm high tide	snowshoe ski lift snowman skating rink
drugstore shopping center parking lot grocery cart	checkbook bank account automatic teller machine deposit slip	passport luggage cart boarding pass window seat

Mime Card Game 2, Compound Nouns *Harder*

fireplace coat hook light switch doorknob	wildfire flash flood landslide climate change	hockey puck chest protector field goal backboard
land mine gunship tank destroyer hand grenade	couch potato chain smoker binge drinker overeater	sightseeing window shopping jaywalking pedestrian crossing
coffee cup frying pan toaster oven tablespoon	seaweed beach towel lifeguard sunburn	heartache runny nose stiff neck backache
background back burner backfire backlog	cold feet heartburn bellyache athlete's foot	daylight leap year weekend afternoon
rolller coaster merry-go-round seesaw water slide	cement mixer dump truck earth mover bulldozer	jellyfish sea lion sand shark brook trout

Mime Card Game 3, Idioms with B

(to) eat like a bird to drop the ball (on) the back burner	on the ball above and beyond (a) backseat driver	(to) back the wrong horse (a) bad hair day go back to the drawing board
(to) bad mouth (someone) (to) bait and switch (a) baker's dozen	(to) leave a bad taste (a) bag of tricks (a) ball of fire	bar none (a) basket case (to) bear down
(to) beat around the bush been there, done that (to) beg, borrow, or steal	(to) beat a dead horse (to) beg the question beside the point	(the) best of both worlds (to) bog down better safe than sorry
(to) bone up on better late than never (to) read between the lines	(a) big fish in a small pond (to) break even (a) big wheel	(the) bitter end (a) blank check between a rock and a hard place
(to) blow off steam by and large (to) break the ice	(to) blow one's mind (a) breath of fresh air (to) bring home the bacon	(to) blow one's top (to) bring to mind both feet on the ground

Mime Card Game 4, Proverbs and Sayings

A bird in the hand is worth two in the bush.	Too many cooks spoil the both.
Don't bite the hand that feeds you.	If the shoe fits, wear it.
Don't throw the baby out with the bath water.	Don't put the cart before the horse.
Make hay while the sun shines.	You can't teach an old dog new tricks.
Let sleeping dogs lie.	The early bird catches the worm.
Don't count your chickens before they hatch.	Two heads are better than one.

Mime Card Game 4, Proverbs and Sayings

A rolling stone gathers no moss.	Don't put all your eggs in one basket.
Don't cry over spilled milk.	Look before you leap.
Practice what you preach.	Where there's smoke, there's fire.
Don't judge a book by its cover.	Actions speak louder than words.
Rome was not built in a day.	One good turn deserves another.
He who hesitates is lost.	A little learning is a dangerous thing.

Conversocards

Brief Description

Pairs of cards each have separate halves of an open-ended conversation. The students begin by saying the given lines to each other. The lines lead the conversation in a general direction, but leave the students to carry on the conversation and bring it to a conclusion.

Purpose

To practice conversation within a semi-controlled communicative context. There is some controlled use of conversation openers, with opportunities to use continuers and closers, employing strategic competence.

Preparation

The cards are used as pairs, so it is advisable to number and letter them: 1A, 1B and 2A, 2B, and so on. On the cards, use blanks (_____) to signify that the speaker should supply some information, and use three dots (. . .) to indicate that the students need to continue the conversation from this point.

Procedure

1. Explain the nature of the activity – that students will work in pairs and each student will receive half of an incomplete conversation, and they have to finish the conversation.

2. Establish a time limit. It will depend on the proficiency level of your students.

3. Divide the class into pairs. If there is an odd number, appoint an official "eavesdropper."

4. Give each pair its pair of cards, and tell them they should not look at each other's cards. If there is a general context to the cards (friends, classmates, workplace, etc.), tell the students what it is. Tell them that the person with the A card will start first. Have the students carry out their conversations. Circulate and eavesdrop, and be available for "How do you say" questions.

5. At the end of the time limit, choose or get volunteers to replay their conversation as the rest of the class watches and listens.

Variations

1. Have each pair work on the same pair of cards, and then compare results by having one pair tell another pair how their conversation went.

2. The students can first write out the continuation of the conversation and then speak and perform it – or write it out afterwards

3. After doing the paired conversation once, take the cards away and have the students perform it from memory.

4. Have one pair perform their conversation and the rest of the class take notes on its direction and conclusion. Then ask the listeners to report the conversation (using reported speech) as the originators listen and correct.

5. Have one pair go through their conversation line by line as you constantly ask the class, "How else could she have said that?" or "Could he say that another way?"

Suggestions

1. **In the classroom***

2. **On the street** (first lines only)
   Can you tell me how to get to _____?
   Where's the nearest _____?
   Is this the road to _____?
   Where do I pay a parking fine?
   Can you tell me which bus _____?
   Taxi!

3. **On the town**

   Do you have any rooms?   What size do you take?
   Would you like a drink before you order?   I'd like to exchange this _____.
   Can you call a cab for me?   I'd like two tickets to _____.
   Waiter, I think you've made a mistake.   I'd like to send this package to _____.
   Will this be cash or charge?   I'm looking for a good used car.
   I have a problem with my car.   I've been having a problem with one
   I'd like to open a checking account.   of my teeth.

4. **In the dorm**

   Turn down the stereo.   Could I wear your sweater today?
   Wake up; you're snoring.   I can't find my room key.
   Shh. Think I heard something.   What time will you be back?
   I'm expecting a phone call at 3 a.m.   I'm going away for the weekend.
   Do you mind if I bring a friend over?   Do you want to send out for pizza?
   Have you seen my toothbrush?   Could you lend me twenty dollars?

* *See sample games on the following pages.*

Conversocards 1, Classroom context

1A 1. Excuse me, could I have a piece of paper? 2. It doesn't matter. 3. Well, I really need . . .	1B 1. Sure. What kind do you want? 2. Will _____ be OK? 3. . . .
2A 1. Excuse me, could you lend me a pencil? 2. I'd prefer a _____ if you have one. 3. In that case . . .	2B 1. Of course. How about a pen? 2. I'm sorry, I only have one pencil, and I may need it. 3. . . .
3A 1. Did you get the homework assignment? 2. What was it? 3. I hope it's not very long.	3B 1. Yes, I think so. 2. It's in my notes. Let me take a look. 3. . . .
4A 1. Would you do a favor for me? 2. Well I need somebody to _____,	4B 1. That depends. What is it? 2. Hmm. So you want somebody to . . .
5A 1. Let's meet at (place) to talk about _____. 2. How about _____? 3. So let's make it _____. 4. . . .	5B 1. Sounds good to me. What time? 2. Oh, I have _____, which lasts until _____. 3. OK. You won't be late, will you?
6A 1. Do you want to work together this evening? 2. OK, where do we meet? 3. We could do that, or we could meet _____.	6B 1. Yeah, that's a good idea. 2. How about _____? 3. That's possible; which . . .

Conversocards 1, Classroom context

7A 1. What's the matter? 2. (Do) you want me to take a look? 3. What do you think it is?	**7B** 1. I think I've got something in my eye. 2. OK, if you don't mind. 3. I think it might be . . .
8A 1. What a nice _____! 2. Where did you get it?	**8B** 1. Thanks, I like it too. 2. I got _____.
9A 1. What are you looking for? 2. That's too bad. Can I help you? 3. What does it look like?	**9B** 1. I lost my _____. 2. Sure. I think it may be _____. 3. Well, it's . . .
10A 1. Excuse me, I'm looking for _____. 2. I said _____. 3. . . .	**10B** 1. I'm sorry, I didn't understand. 2. It's noisy in here. Could you say that again?
11A 1. Did you see/watch/listen to _____ last night? 2. Well, I thought . . .	**11B** 1. No, I didn't. How was it? 2. Really? So it sounds like . . .
12A 1. Have you made any plans for the weekend? 2. I was thinking that maybe you and I could _____. 3. Well . . .	**12B** 1. No, not yet. Why? 2. Hmm. Tell me more.

Conversocards 2, At a coffee shop with a friend

1A 　1. I'm buying today. 　2. Sorry, I owe you. 　3. Remember, last week you . . .	1B 　1. No way. It's my turn. 　2. What for? 　3. OK. Then I'll have . . .
2A 　1. What'll you have? 　2. Leave room for creamer? 　3. Anything else?	2B 　1. I'll have a medium. 　2. _____. 　3. . . .
3A 　1. Hey (name), what are you doing here? 　2. So, how's it going? 　3. Cool, can I join you?	3B 　1. I'm just _____. 　2. Not bad, I'm . . . 　3. . . .
4A 　1. (name), have you heard the weather report? 　2. That's _____. 　3. I've got to _____.	4B 　1. Yes I have. It looks like . . . 　2. Why? What's up?
5A 　1. Hi, (name). Do you know where (name) is? 　2. Have you seen him/her today? 　3. Was he/she with somebody? 　4. Well, ...	5B 　1. No, I don't think so. 　2. Let's see. I think I saw him/her at _____. 　3. Umm. Maybe. Why do you ask?
6A 　1. Could I take a look at your newspaper? 　2. The _____ section. 　3. Checking to see ... 　4. Because ...	6B 　1. Yeah, sure. Which section? 　2. OK. Here it is. What are you looking for? 　3. Why are you doing that?

Conversocards 2, At a coffee shop with a friend

7A 1. So, how are things today? 2. How did you get here? 3. I don't know. What time do you get out? 4. Umm. Can you be more specific?	**7B** 1. Not good. My car won't start. 2. I took the bus. Can I get a ride with you after work? 3. Usually by 5 or 5:30.
8A 1. So how are things going? 2. How come? 3. Yeah, so . . ?	**8B** 1. Don't ask. 2. I've got a problem. 3. Well, . . .
9A 1. Do you have your car here? 2. I need a ride. 3. Can you take me to . . . . 4. It's . . .	**9B** 1. Yeah, Why? 2. OK. Where are you going? 3. Where's that?
10A 1. What's up with you for the weekend? 2. How'd you like to . . . . 3. Really? I've got two tickets to the basketball game.	**10B** 1. I don't know (dunno). Nothing much. 2. I think I'll just hang out with (name). 3. You have? Maybe . . .
11A 1. Did you watch TV last night? 2. You missed a really great _____. 3. At ten. 4.	**11B** 1. No, I didn't. 2. When was it on? 3. Anyway, I couldn't have. I was . . .
12A 1. Hi, (name). Where were you yesterday? 2. Well, we missed you. 3. Yeah, (name) was here. 4. Well, he/she said	**12B** 1. I was . . . 2. You did? 3. Oh no, I've been dying to meet him/her.

Instructocards

Brief Description

One student has a card with a set of instructions on it. The student reads the instructions to a second student, who follows the instructions. There can be several types of instructions, from simple body movement to operating a piece of equipment.

Purpose

To practice a connected series of statements and commands, including discourse connectors such as *first, then, after that*, etc., and to use and learn new vocabulary.

Preparation

The cards can be simple or complex, from very short sets of instructions requiring physical activity, to more abstract sequential activities such as "How to sell a car" and "How to apply for a job." Easier sequences should have 5-7 separate instructions, and should have associated physical activity, while more difficult sequences can have longer sentences and 7-10 separate instructions.

Procedure

1. Pair the students and explain the nature of the activity. You can demonstrate, having one student follow your instructions.

2. Give one student in each pair a card with its set of instructions. You can give the same set of instructions to each pair, or you can give each pair a different set of instructions. For the beginning level classes, it may be easier if the entire class is doing the same set of instructions.

3. Ask the students with the cards to study the cards first. If they have any questions, they should check with you now.

4. Have the student with the card look at the first instruction, read it, look up at the other student, and say it.

5. The second student performs the instruction, or if they don't understand, they are allowed to say, "I don't understand." The first student must search for an alternative instruction.

6. When the entire sequence has been done, the students change roles. The listener becomes the instructor, and vice versa. If this is too easy, give the students a new card.

Variations

1. Some kinds of activities can be played as competitive games. For example, the activity can be for the followers on each team to successfully tie a necktie, perhaps while blindfolded.

2. After each step (or after all the steps), the instructor can ask the follower to say what they did.

3. The follower can be allowed to ask questions as the instructions are given.

4. At the end of the activity, both students can be asked to write out the instructions from memory. At this point, you can insist on accuracy. Producing a final, perfect set of instructions can be an all-class activity.

5. Students can make their own instructocards.

6. The followers can be "blind," and the card gives only a destination or goal, toward which the instructor gives the follower instructions. One favorite activity, "Airport," has the instructor (airport tower) "land" the blindfolded "plane" (follower) on a "runway" with obstacles in it.

Suggestions

1. Simple physical movements*
   - go to the board
   - go out of the room
   - retrieve something
   - pick up/take/carry something

2. Simple physical skills
   - sewing on a button
   - brushing teeth
   - shampooing hair

3. Operating a piece of equipment
   - using a camera
   - using machines at a laundromat
   - loading a dishwasher
   - pumping gas
   - driving a car

4. Performing a ritualistic action/procedure
   - going through a cafeteria line
   - a subway ride
   - a bank transaction
   - tuning a guitar
   - formatting a business letter

5. Processes
   - reading effectively
   - doing a research paper
   - preparing food (recipes)
   - transplanting a flower
   - cleaning a fish tank
   - shopping in a supermarket

6. Doing games and exercises
   - card games
   - board games
   - dance steps
   - volleyball, table tennis
   - video games

7. Miscellaneous instructions
   - following a road map*
   - applying for a loan
   - getting a Social Security number
   - registering a car
   - registering to vote
   - running a business meeting

   See sample games on the following pages.

For a good collection of activities, see *Do As I Say* from Pro Lingua Associates.

Instructocards 1, Physical Movement

A. 1. Go to the board. 2. Pick up a marker. 3. Write your full name. 4. Put down the marker. 5. Pick up the eraser. 6. Erase your last/first/middle name. 7. Bring the eraser back to me.	B. 1. Stand up. 2. Walk to the door. 3. Turn out the lights. 4. Open the door. 5. Look outside. 6. Close the door. 7. Turn on the lights. 8. Go back to your seat.
C. 1 Stand up. 2. Stand on one leg. 3. Hop over to the window. 4. Turn around. 5. Change legs. 6. Hop back here. 7. Continue standing for as long as you can.	D. 1. Go over to the wall. 2. Lean your back against the wall. 3. Put both hands on top of your head. 4. Take one hand away. 5. Push away from the wall. 6. Come back.
E. 1. Take my pencil 2. Give it to the teacher. 3. Ask the teacher to give it to _____. 4. Ask _____ to give it to _____. 5. Ask _____ to sharpen the pencil. 6. Tell _____ to give it back to _____ . etc.	F. 1. Open your book. 2. Turn to the exact middle. 3. Look at the page number. 4. Put your pencil in the page. 5. Turn to the last page. 6. Look at the page number. 7. Close the book. 8. Tell me the page numbers.
G. 1. Go over to _____. 2. Take _____'s hand. 3. Lead him/her to the door. 4. Tell him/her to wait there. 5. Go get _____. 6. Lead him/her to _____. 7. Tell _____ to _____.	H. 1. Please begin whistling. 2. Stroll around the room whistling. 3. Go to a window and stop whistling. 4. Look out the window. 5. Open it if you can. 6. Look left and right. 7. Begin humming and come back to me. 8. Stop humming and whisper to me what you did.

Instructocards 1, Physical Movement

I.
1. Go over to _____.
2. Ask him/her to whisper his/her favorite color.
3. Go over to _____.
4. Ask him/her to guess what _____'s favorite color is.
5. If he/she is right, come back. If he/she is wrong, tell _____ to go ask _____.
6. Come back and tell me _____'s favorite color.

J.
1. Get up slowly and tiptoe out of the room.
2. Wait! When you get there, wait five seconds.
3. Then rush in, get your books, and rush out.
4. Wait for me outside.
.... (Go outside) ....
5. OK, give me your books.
6. Now go back in, get my books, and come back.
7. Good. Now take all the books back and go to your seat.

K.
1. Go outside. Wait! I'm coming with you.
2. OK, let's walk down the hallway.
3. Stop at this door.
4. What's inside?
5. Let's turn around.
6. Tell me where you want to go.
7. OK, let's go.

L.
1. Would you please come here and stand in front of me.
2. Now take off my wrist watch.
3. Find another watch or clock and check the time.
4. Go to the board and write either. "Your watch is too slow," or "Your watch is too fast."
5. Thanks. Now please bring my watch back and put it on my wrist.

M.
1. Take this coin.
2. I'm going to close my eyes.
3. Hide the coin somewhere.
4. After you have hidden it, tell me to open my eyes.
5. Answer my questions with "cold," "cool," "warm," "hot," and "red hot" until I find it.
....
6. OK, I found it. Now you close your eyes, etc.

N.
1. Walk over to that corner and wait for me.
2. OK. Now that we're both in this corner, walk back to your seat, but don't sit down.
3. After you get there, pick up your stuff and wait for me.
4. Good! Now change seats with me.
5. Thank you! Let's sit down.

O.
1. Please go over to the window.
2. When you get there, find five things to talk about.
....
3. OK! Come on back.
4. Tell me what you saw, and answer my questions.
5. Good! Now tell me to go to another window, and you do what I did.

P.
1. Please take off your _____.
2. Now give it to _____, and come back.
3. Tell me what you did.
4. What did _____ say?
5. Now go back and get your _____, and give it to _____.
6. Tell me what you did.

126

Instructocards 2, Following a Road Map

In this game a pair of students each have the same map. One student begins with:

You are at (the junction of routes 10 and 89).
Go south until you come to XXXXX, etc. etc.

Finally the instructor checks to see where the follower really is.

San Antonio, TX Area

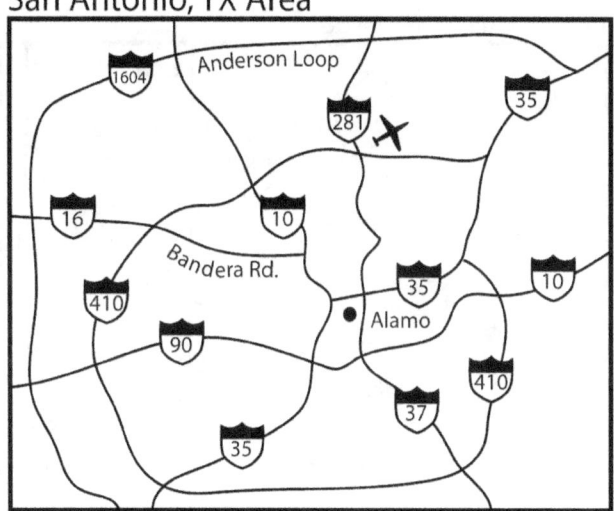

Tucson, AZ Area

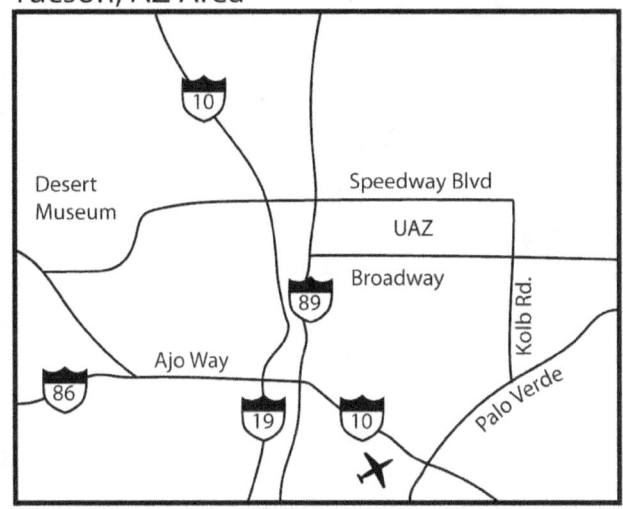

Las Vegas, NV Area

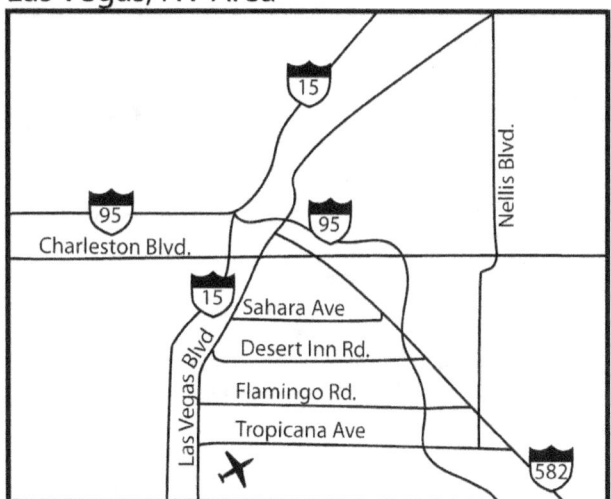

Albuquerque, NM Area

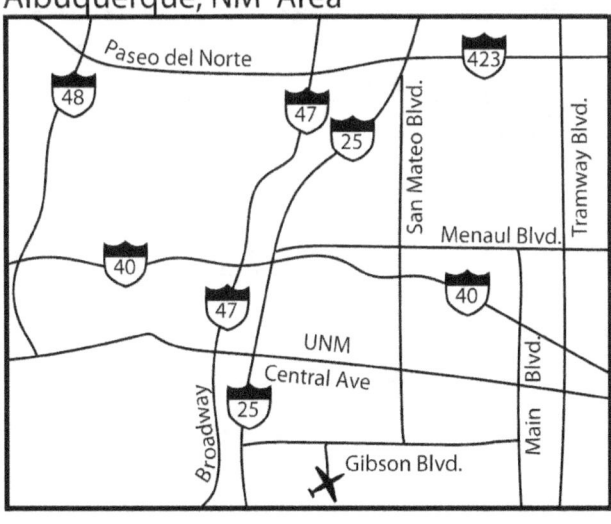

Anaheim, CA Area

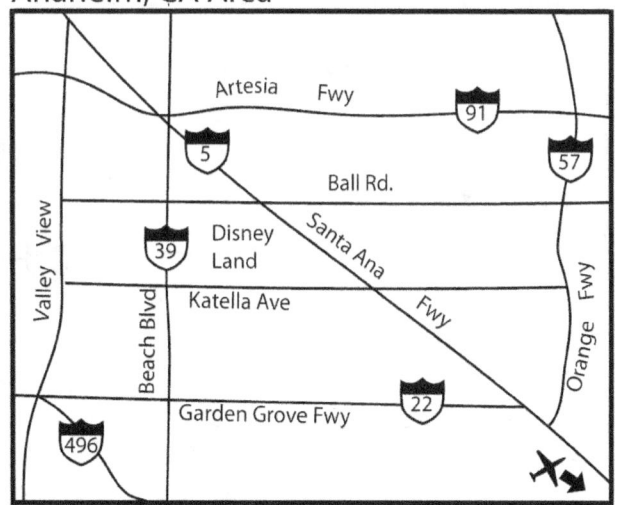

Instructocards 2, Following a Road Map

Des Moines, IA Area

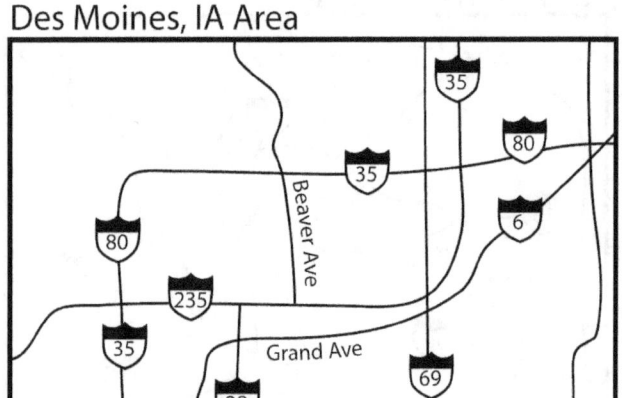

Kansas City, KS-MO Area

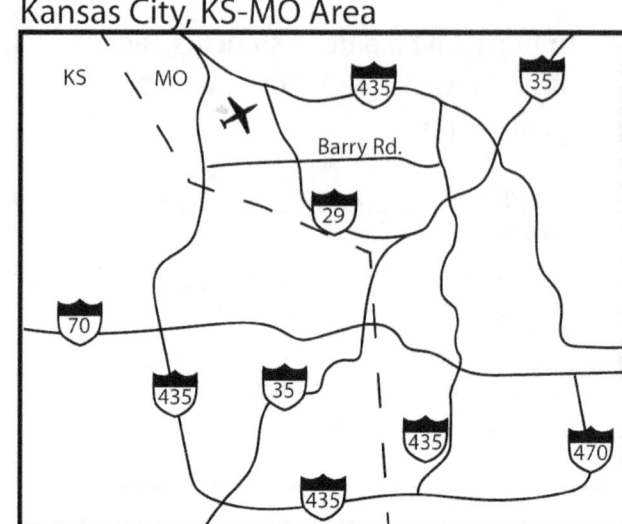

Minneapolis, MN Area

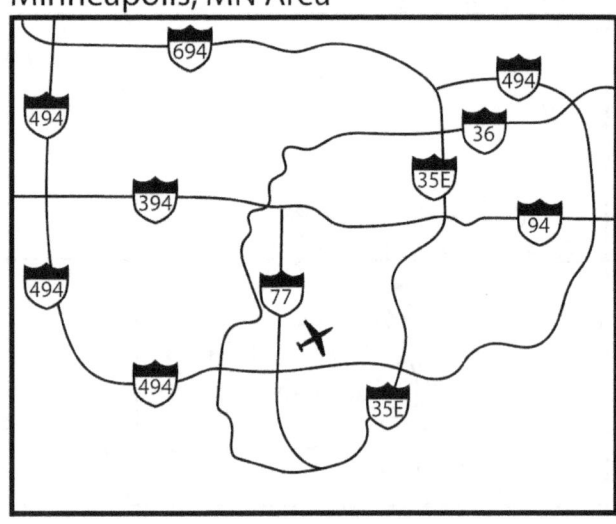

St. Louis MO-IL Area

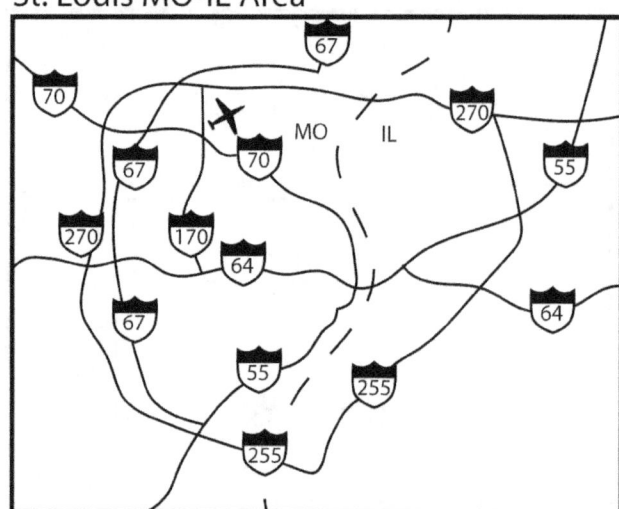

Indianapolis, IN Area

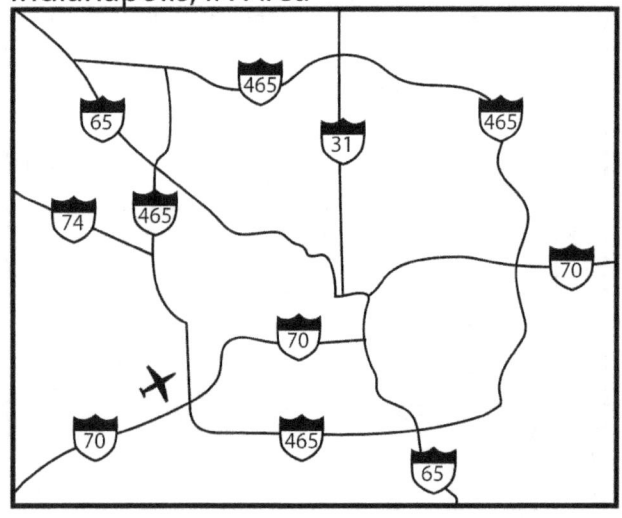

Orlando, FL Area

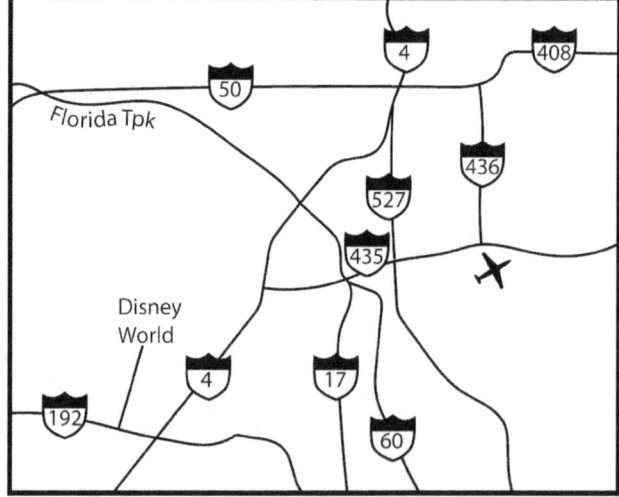

Instructocards 2, Following a Road Map

Columbus, OH Area
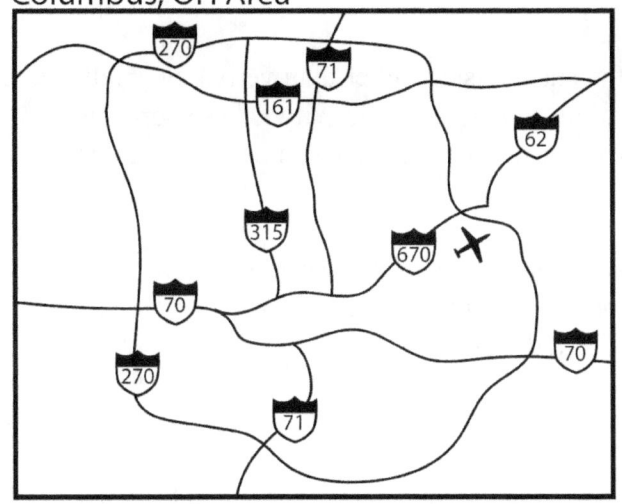

Atlanta, GA Area
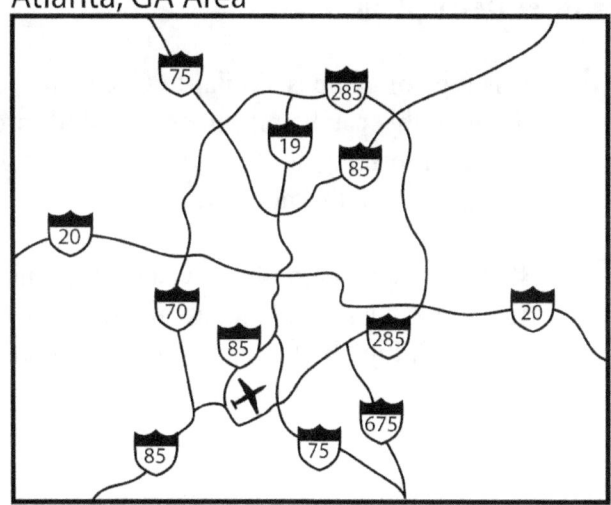

Philadelphia, PA Area
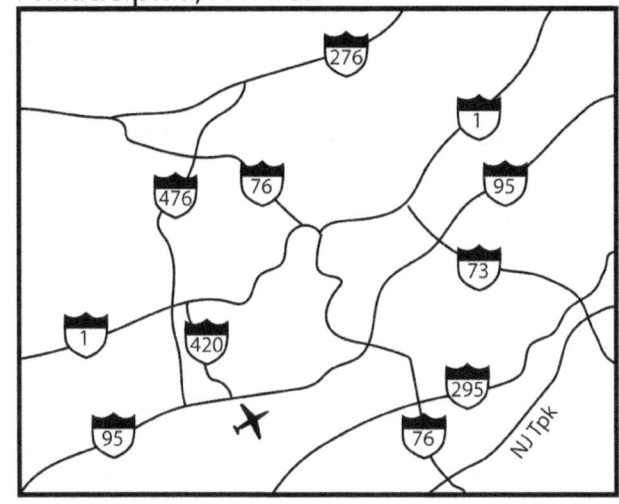

Baltimore, MD Area
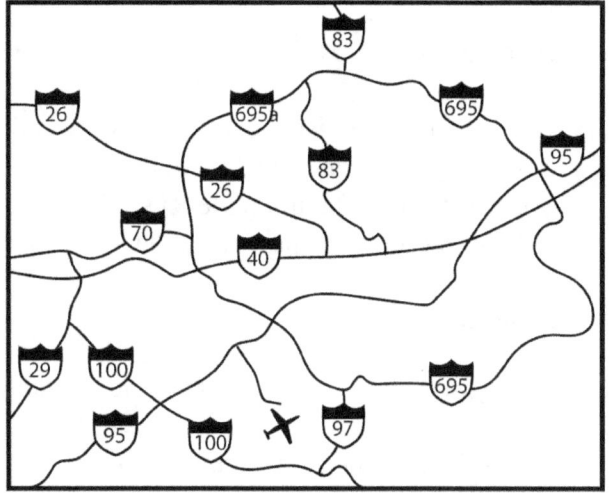

Hartford, CT Area
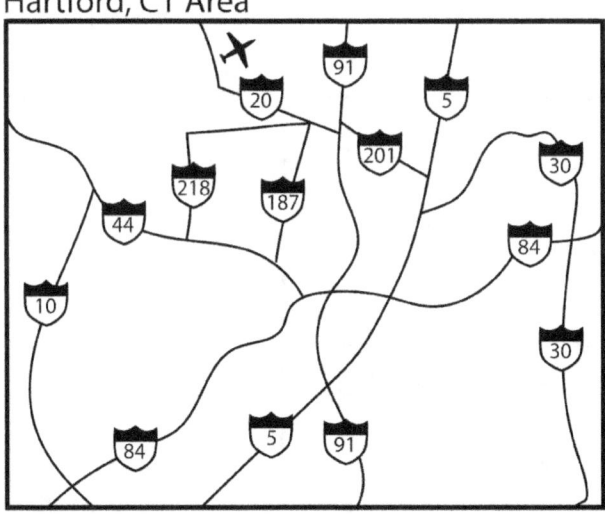

Boston, MA Area
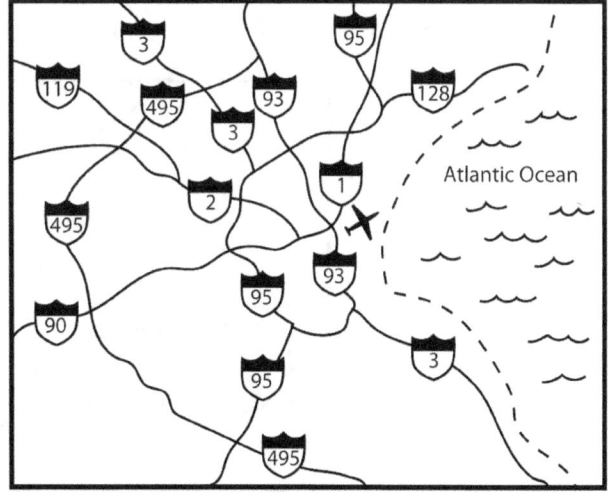

Pictograms

Brief Description

This type of game is similar to Cue Cards, but the cue is visual rather than verbal. Secondly, although this can be played as a kind of information exchange, the activity is based on one student informing another student accurately. In other words, accuracy can be more important than fluency in this activity.

Student A has a card with a visual stimulus. The student describes the card to Student B, who tries to form a mental picture and/or draw a sketch on a blank card of what was described. Finally the two pictures are compared and discussed.

Purpose

To sharpen the students' skill at expressing themselves with considerable detail and accuracy. The activity can also be used to practice question-answer exchange, and it can be a good exercise for introducing and using new vocabulary.

Preparation

The number of visual cues is virtually endless -- old magazines are an excellent source. Although the standard 3 x 5 index cards can be used, complex pictures may require a larger format. Beginning level students should not be given visual cues that have a lot of detail requiring a large vocabulary.

Procedure

The procedure below is very basic; it can be used with beginners and advanced students.

1. Pair the students and explain the nature of the game. If possible, have the students sit back to back so that the listener cannot easily see the speaker.

2. Give one of the students in each pair the pictogram. For beginners, use about 5-8 very simple items in the pictogram, as in the example below.

3. Give the other half of each pair a blank piece of paper and pencil and eraser. You may also want to establish a time limit at this point: 4-8 minutes should be enough.

4. The student with the pictogram describes the picture, and the other student attempts to draw it on their piece of paper. They may converse back and forth.

5. Give a one-minute warning before the end of the time limit, and then stop everybody. Collect the drawings and post them or put them on a large table. Number each one.

6. Have all the students examine the exhibit of drawings and select the one that comes closest to the original that was described to them.

Variations

1. One way to vary the game is to use different kinds of visual cues. One type that is commonly used is a sheet of stiff paper, colored on one side.

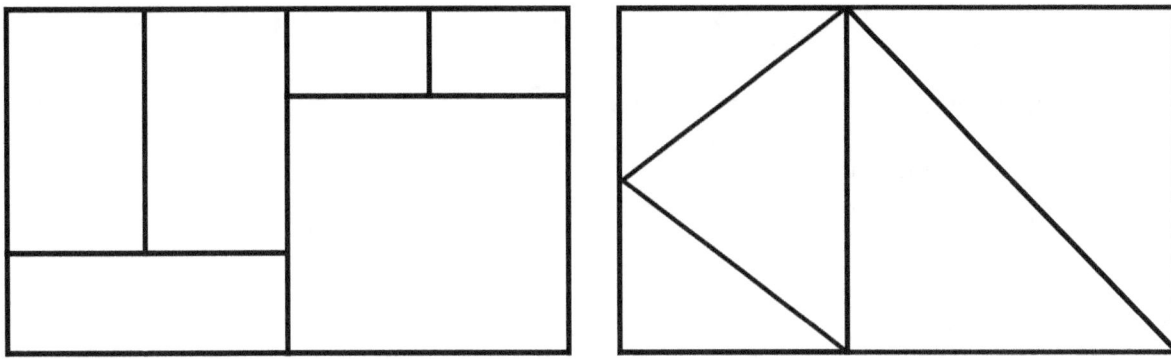

2. Make two copies of the picture for each pair. One student has a card with the complete picture. The other gets an envelope that contains the picture cut up into pieces. The student with the solution instructs the other student on how to assemble the pieces. One variation of this procedure is to give both students duplicate envelopes with shapes that can be assembled into any pattern. One arranges and describes a pattern while the second listens and attempts to duplicate it.

3. Another variation is to use objects such as children's blocks, Legos, Cuisenaire rods, or some other set of objects.

4. To make the game more challenging, the listener can be restricted to:
    ● asking only yes/no questions
    ● responding to the speaker with yes or no
    ● no talking

5. One interesting variation is to use a set of pictures that are similar, but all slightly different – For example, postcards with different views of the Golden Gate Bridge. Each pair gets a different card. One student describes the picture while the other listens, picturing it in their

mind or trying to draw it. After a short time limit, tell all the groups to stop and put the picture face down without showing it to their partner. Collect the cards and put them on a table top or a chalk tray. Invite the listeners to come and choose the picture that was described to them. They bring their choice back to the describer to see if they are right (it helps to give the describer two identical pictures as they may not remember every detail of the picture they described). If the listener is not right, they take it back or look for another person who has their card.

6. Similar to variation 5, this variation is done with real pictures that may be much bigger than index cards. Collect a set of pictures that show a scene, but are all slightly different. Calendar pictures may also work if they all portray a similar scene, such as mountains, beaches, flowers, or birds.

Suggestions

1. Simple sketches*

2. Objects

    - different ballpoint pens

    - small toy automobiles (Hot Wheels)

    - plastic animals, bugs, dinosaurs

3. Postcards

4. Postage stamps

5. Clothing catalogs

6 Pictures from magazines

7. Maps in Instructocards

8. National flags*

9. Houses (See real estate listings in Cue Cards.)

* *See sample games on the following pages*

Pictograms 1, Desktop

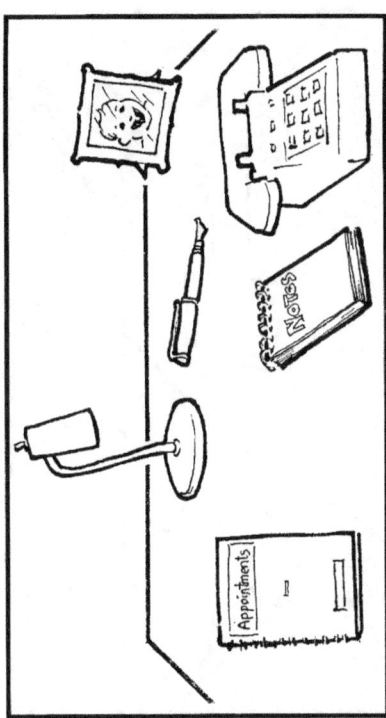
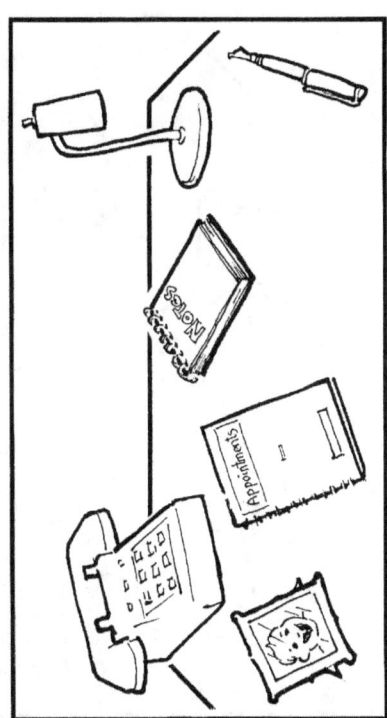

Pictograms 1, Desktop

Pictograms 2, National Flags *Horizontal*

National Flags

This easy game requires only that the students identify the stripes as vertical or horizontal and the colors. *Left, right, center*, and prepositions may also be necessary.

To make the game a little more challenging, the listeners do not draw as they listen. They have to commit the description to memory, and then try to find the flag that was described.

There are several sites on the Internet where you may download the flags in color. An alternative is to color one set with colored pencils or crayons for the teller, and have the listeners color the flag as they listen.

After the game, you can give the students the key below with the names of the countries.

Country Key

Horizontal Stripes
- a. Hungary
- b. Gabon
- c. Netherlands
- d. Yemen
- e. Luxembourg
- f. Sierra Leone
- g. Germany
- h. Bulgaria
- i. Bolivia
- j. Russia

Vertical Stripes
- k. Guinea
- l. Ivory Coast
- m. Canary Islands
- n. Belgium
- o. Mali
- p. France
- q. Chad
- r. Ireland
- s. Romania
- t. Italy

Pictograms 2, National Flags *Horizontal stripes*

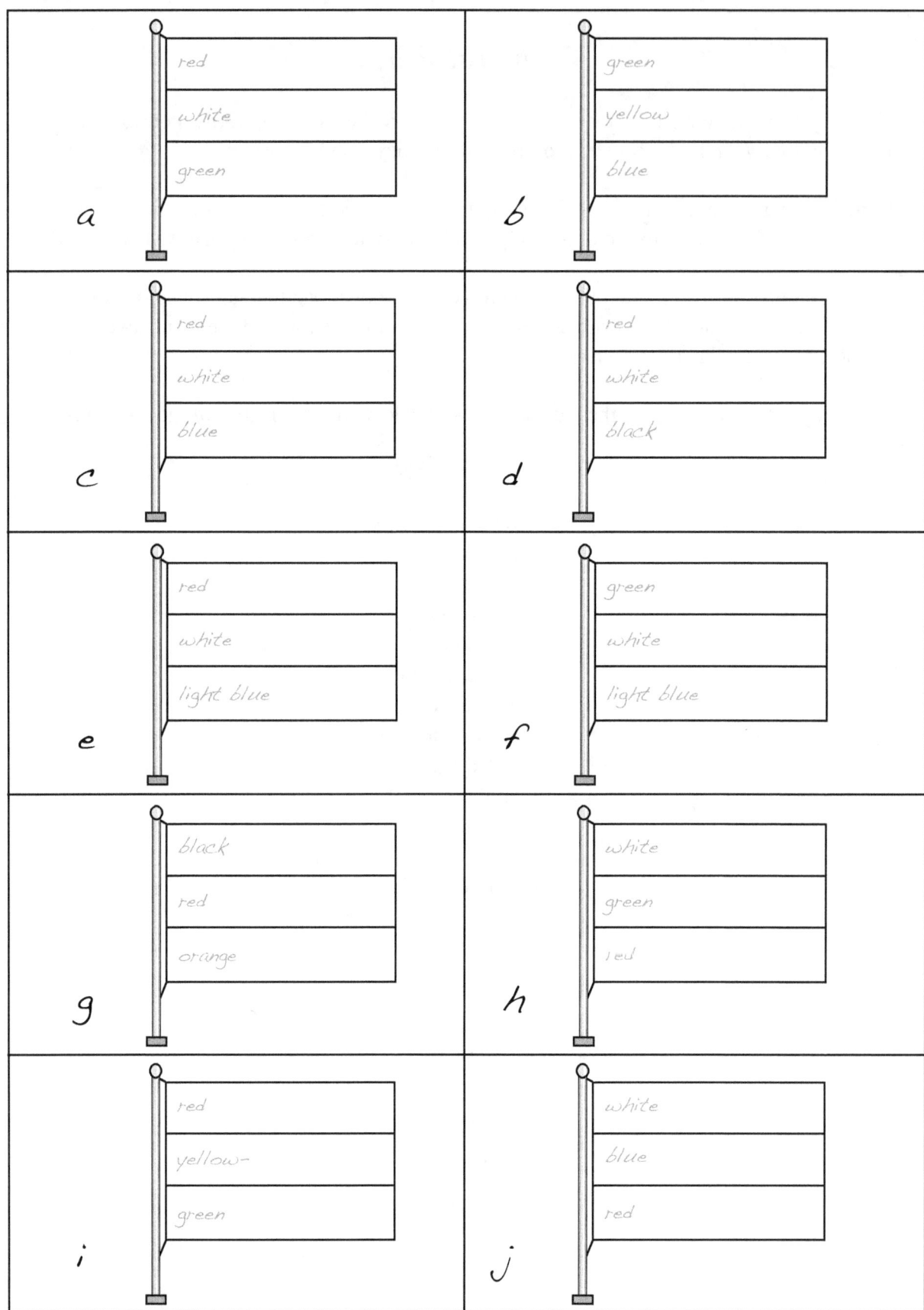

Pictograms 2, National Flags *Vertical stripes*

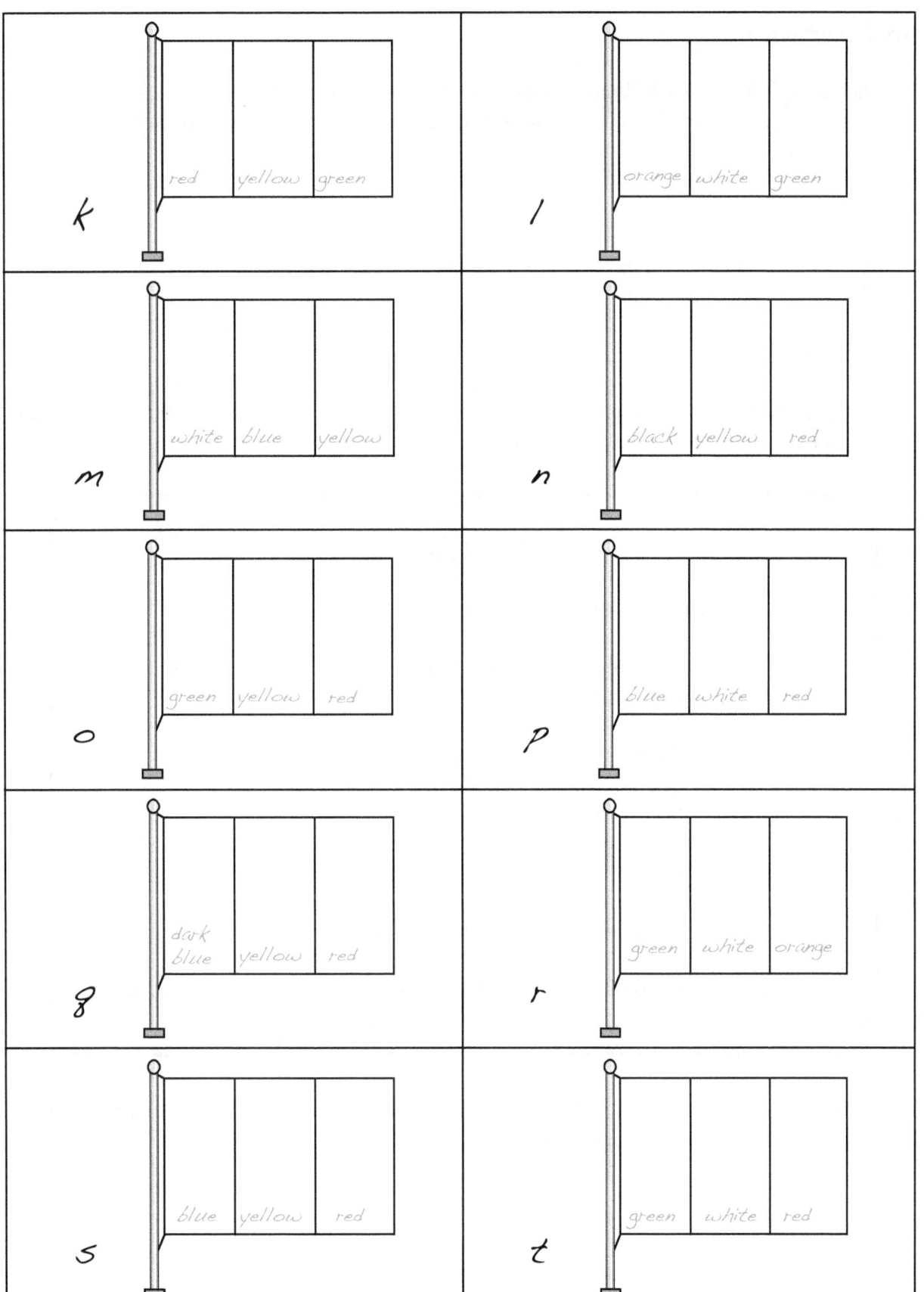

Line Up

Brief Description

Each student is given a different piece of information. Each piece is part of a list that needs to be arranged in a specific order. The students line up, trying to put themselves in the specified order.

Purpose

Conversation practice. To have the students talk with each other to find the solution, and afterwards discuss the results.

Preparation

First prepare a master list that is the list of each item (card) in the correct order. Also give the instructions on the master list. For example:

Animal Speeds

How fast can animals go at top speed for a short distance?

Each of you has a card with an animal's name on it. Line up from fastest to slowest, with the fastest here and the slowest there.

Animal	Speed (mph)
Falcon	200+ mph
Cheetah	70
Pronghorn antelope	61
Lion	50
Horse	47.5
Coyote	43

Etc. See Sample Game #1 for complete game.

Source: *Natural History Magazine*, 1974, and http://www.factmonster.com

---

Then prepare a series of cards. For most games 16 different cards is about maximum. More than that can become confusing.

Procedure

1. Copy the master list for yourself, and make one copy for each student, to be used in step 8.

2. Give each student a card. Check to be sure that the students know the vocabulary of the items that will be arranged. Ten to twelve items seem to work best, but with some groups, up to 16 different items is possible. Make sure the cards are distributed in random order. You may want to appoint a "line captain" – see step 5. Then give the instructions on the master list.

3. Have each student announce the name on their card.

4. Have the students stand up and begin moving into place as they talk to each other. Caution: If the students all have the same native language, be sure they don't start using their native language. Make this prohibition clear before you begin.

5. If the number of students exceeds the number of cards, some students can be a pair. If there are not many students, some students can have two cards. If you have a "line captain": when the group seems to be nearing a solution, the captain can step outside the line and urge the group to reach their solution, perhaps offering comments.

6. Have the students say their cards in order. Depending on the proficiency of the group, they can also explain their reasons for their placement.

7. Read the answers and have them move if necessary.

8. If there is additional information (such as actual animal speeds in the sample), they can try to guess the additional information.

9. Hand out the master list and have the students return to their places for a general discussion, if relevant, starting off with "What surprised you?"

Variations

1. With a large class, have two groups of students make two lines (You need to prepare a duplicate set of cards). When they are ready, have them compare their lines and discuss differences. Finally, supply the answers.

2. With a small class, the students can lay their cards out in a line on a table top or in the whiteboard marker tray, or write them on the board.

Suggestions

1. The cost of things
    - cars
    - TVs
    - computers
    - phones
    - houses (real estate ads without prices – see Cue Cards)
    - food, per pound (unit pricing)

2. Distances of places from the classroom
    - in the town/city
    - in the state
    - in the country
    - in the world

3. Population figures
    - towns/cities in the state
    - states in the country
    - countries in the world
    - population density

4. Nutritional value of foods
    - protein
    - fiber
    - vitamin content
    - sugar content
    - carbohydrate content

5. Geographical information
    - lengths of rivers
    - heights of mountains
    - land area of countries
    - sizes of bodies of water

6. Historical information
    - sequence of events
    - size of disasters

Notes

1. This activity lends itself to practicing comparative and superlative constructions.

2. Line ups are often used as ice breakers or warm ups.

Line Ups 1, Animal Speeds — Master List

Animal Speeds

How fast can animals go at top speed for a short distance?

Each of you has a card with an animal's name on it. Line up from fastest to slowest, with the fastest here and the slowest there. First, tell everybody what animal you have.

Animal	MPH
Peregrine Falcon	200+
Cheetah	70
Pronghorn Antelope	61
Lion	50
Horse	47.5
Coyote	43
Ostrich	40
Greyhound	37.5
House Cat	35
Rabbit (Domestic)	35
Giraffe	32
Kangaroo	30
Grizzly Bear	30
White-tailed Deer	30
Human	27.89
Elephant	25
Black Mamba Snake	20
Six-lined Race Runner Lizard	18
Squirrel	12
Chicken	9
House Mouse	8
Giant Tortoise	0.17
Three-toed Sloth	0.15

Note: There are 23 cards in this list, but on the following pages the cards are divided into two lists of 12 each, and "Human" is included in each list. Therefore you can play two games of 12 cards each or select up to 16 (the recommended maximum number) from the two lists.

Source: *Natural History Magazine,* 1974 and Http://WWW.factmonster.co

Line Ups 1, Animal Speeds — Game Cards

Peregrine Falcon	**Cheetah**
Pronghorn Antelope	**Lion**
Horse	Coyote
Ostrich	Greyhound
Giraffe	House Cat
Rabbit (Domestic)	Human

Line Ups 1, Animal Speeds *Game Cards*

Kangaroo	Grizzly Bear
White-tailed Deer	Human
Elephant	Black Mamba Snake
Six-lined Race Runner Lizard	Squirrel
Chicken	House Mouse
Giant Tortoise	Three-toed Sloth

Line Ups 2, Decomposability *Master List*

Decomposability

How fast do things decompose?
To decompose means to decay from an original thing to something like dust.

Each of you has a card with a name of a thing on it. Some of these things decompose very quickly. Some take a long time. Line up from fastest to slowest to decompose, with the fastest here and the slowest there. First tell everybody what item you have.

Object	Time to Decompose
paper towel	2-4 weeks
banana peel	3-4 weeks
paper bag	1 month
newspaper	1.5 months
apple core	2 months
cardboard	2 months
orange peel	6 months
plywood	1-3 years
wool sock	1-5 years
milk carton	5 years
cigarette butt	10-12 years
leather shoe	25-40 years
aluminum can	200-500 years
plastic bag	200-1000 years
plastic bottle	450 years – forever
disposable diaper	550 years

Source: www.hoaxorfact.com/science/how-long-does-it-take-to-decompose.html

Note: Another similar term is "biodegrade." This means the thing decays into organic matter.

Line ups 2, Decomposability *Game Cards*

paper towel	banana peel
paper bag	newspaper
apple core	cardboard
orange peel	plywood

Line ups 2, Decomposability *Game Cards*

wool sock	milk carton
cigarette butt	leather shoe
aluminum can	plastic bag
plastic bottle	disposable diaper

Line Ups 3, Protein Content — *Master List*

Protein Content

How much protein do different kinds of food contain?

Each of you has a card with a name of a food on it. Some of these foods have a lot of protein per 100 grams; some do not have much protein. Arrange yourself in a line from here to there according to how much protein your food contains per 100 grams. In some cases, these foods may have the same amount of protein. First tell everybody what food you have.

Protein Content. Grams of protein per 100 grams

36	Lean Beef
32	Nonfat Mozzarella Cheese
32	Peanuts
32	Almonds
30	Turkey Breast
30	Chicken Breast
26	Tuna
26	Salmon
25	Pork Loin
17	Soybeans
17	White Beans
13	Eggs
7	Tofu
6	Yogurt
6	Milk
6	Soy Milk

Source: www.Healthaliciousness.com

Line Ups 3, Protein Content *Game Cards*

Lean Beef	Non-Fat Mozzarella Cheese
Peanuts	Almonds
Turkey Breast	Chicken Breast
Tuna	Salmon

Line Ups 3, Protein Content *Game Cards*

Pork Loin	Soy Beans
White Beans	Eggs
Tofu	Yogurt
Milk	Soy Milk

Line Ups 4, Largest Countries by Population *Master List*

Largest Countries by Population

What are the world's 16 largest countries in population?

Each of you has a card with a name of a country on it. Arrange yourself in a line according to the size of the country's population. The highest population here, and the lowest there. First tell everybody what country you have.

World's 16 Largest Countries by Population (Millions)

China	1,361,500
India	1,251,700
United States	322,400
Indonesia	255,750
Brazil	212,350
Pakistan	199,050
Nigeria	183,500
Bangladesh	168,950
Russia	136,100
Japan	126,900
Mexico	118,700
Philippines	109,600
Ethiopia	103,100
Vietnam	94,350
Egypt	88,500
Turkey	82,500

Source: www.geoba.com (2015 estimate)

Line Ups 4, Largest Countries by Population *Game Cards*

China	India
United States	Indonesia
Brazil	Pakistan
Nigeria	Bangladesh

Line Ups 4, Largest Countries by Population *Game Cards*

Russia	**Japan**
Mexico	**Philippines**
Ethiopia	**Vietnam**
Egypt	**Turkey**

Line Ups 5, Selected World Cities by Population *Master List*

Selected World Cities by Population

Each of you has a card with a name of a city on it. Arrange yourself in a line according to the size of the city proper's population. "Proper" means only the city, not the metropolitan area. These are selected cities, not the 16 largest. Now arrange yourselves according to the highest population, with the highest here, and the lowest there. First tell everybody what city you have.

Selected Cities (not top 16), in Millions

Shanghai	24,500
Karachi	23,500
Beijing	21,516
Delhi	17,839
Lagos	17,060
Istanbul	14,160
Mumbai	12,655
Moscow	12,111
Dhaka	12,044
Sao Paulo	11,986
Cairo	11,923
Seoul	10,388
Tokyo	9,071
Mexico City	8,875
London	8,416
New York	8,405

Source: Wikipedia. United Nations City Proper List

Line Ups 5, Selected World Cities by Populations *Game Cards*

Shanghai	Karachi
Beijing	Delhi
Lagos	Istanbul
Mumbai	Moscow

Line Ups 5, Selected World Cities by Populations *Game Cards*

Dhaka	**Cairo**
Sao Paulo	**Seoul**
Tokyo	**Mexico City**
London	**New York**

Line Ups 4, Largest Countries by Land Area *Master List*

Largest Countries by Land Area

What are 16 largest countries in land area?

Each of you has a card with a name of a country on it. Arrange yourself in a line according to the size of these countries' land areas. The largest area here, and the lowest there. First, tell everybody what country you have.

Country	Square Kilometers (nearest hundreds)
Russia	16,377,700
China	9,569,900
United States	9,162,000
Canada	9,093,500
Brazil	8,459,400
Australia	7,682,300
India	2,973,200
Argentina	2,736,700
Kazakhstan	2,699,700
Algeria	2,381,700
Democratic Republic of Congo	2,267,000
Saudi Arabia	2,149,700
Mexico	1,943,900
Sudan	1,861,500
Indonesia	1,811,700
Libya	1,759,500

Source: http://world.bymap.org/LandArea.html

Line Ups 6, Largest Countries by Land Area   *Game Cards*

Russia	**China**
United States	**Canada**
Brazil	**Australia**
India	**Argentina**

Line Ups 4, Largest Countries by Land Area *Game Cards*

Kazakhstan	**Algeria**
Democratic Republic of Congo	**Saudi Arabia**
Mexico	**Sudan**
Indonesia	**Libya**

Finder Cards

Brief Description

This is a role-playing exercise in which each student receives a card that requires them to mingle with the other participants and accomplish some kind of objective that is spelled out at the beginning of the game. Often the objective is to find information or a solution to a problem. The well-known "Find Someone Who" game is a basic version of this activity.

Purpose

Conversation practice. The activity requires the students to elicit and give information by listening carefully and speaking accurately.

Preparation

It is recommended that you have no more than 16 players (although a pair of students can be one "player". A basic pattern for creating an 8-person game is to have 16 pieces of information and for each card to have on it four pieces of information. The arrangement below establishes that each player will have only one piece of information in common with any other player. Thus, if Student 1 is looking for four pieces of information (A, B, I, M) they will have to encounter several other students to get all the information because only four other students will have A, or B or I or M, and several students (Student 3, for example) will not have the information.

Student	*Information*
1	A B I M
2	B C J N
3	C D K O
4	D E L P
5	E F I O
6	F G J P
7	G H K M
8	H A L N

Procedure

1. Using the master list, explain the nature of the game.

2. Give the cards to the students, and give them time to clarify the information on the card and the procedure to follow.

3. Let the students mingle and talk to each other. Fifteen minutes is usually sufficient. Try to have the students use the entire available area rather than bunching up. It is sometimes useful to station half of the group, and have the other half move from station to station.

4. When it seems the game is winding down, conclude it and have the students go back to their seats.and report on what they found and who had the information.

Variations

1. A competitive element can be added by having the students call out "DONE!" when they have found everything they needed.

2. Encourage the students to share information with each other, for example:

   Maria: Ahmed, have you been to Cyprus?
   Ahmed: No, I haven't visited Cyprus, but I think Jorge has."

3. You can have the students create their own four-item card using one of the suggested topics below. "Favorites" would be good for this variation – for example, "four favorite vacation spots."

Suggestions

1. Island hopping *
2. Countries visited
3. Cities visited
4. Airlines flown
5. Languages spoken
6. Translator needed
7. Currency exchange *
8. Witness to major event
9. Timeshare swap *
10. Favorites
    Vegetables and fruits *
    Vacation spots *
    Leisure activities
    Colors
    Animals
    Automobiles
    Flowers
    Sports*

Note: A sample completed card from game 1, "Island Hoppers"

Island	Your Rating	Visitors & Rating
Cuba	**	*Juan* **
Grenada	*	*Raouf* **
Rhodes	***	*Dao* ***
Vanuatu	**	*Sema* *

Finder Cards 1, Island Hoppers *Master List*

Island Hoppers

You are a member of the Island Hoppers Club and you are at the annual meeting of the club. Meet other members and find out who has been to the four islands that you have visited. (Optionally), ask them how they rated their visit (1- 4 stars). Collect their opinions of the four islands, and on your own card write 1 - 4 stars on your opinion of the island. Be prepared to explain your rating (use your imagination). When you have found one other person who has visited each of your four islands, go back to your seat.

Finally everybody will share their information.

But first, let's locate these islands on a map. Here are the 16 islands

        A. Cuba

        B. Grenada

        C. Puerto Rico

        D. Bermuda

        E. Madagascar

        F. Zanzibar

        G. Sardinia

        H. Sicily

        I. Rhodes

        J. Cyprus

        K. Fiji

        L. Tahiti

        M. Vanuatu

        N. Guam

        O. Bali

        P. Tasmania

The Island Hoppers' World

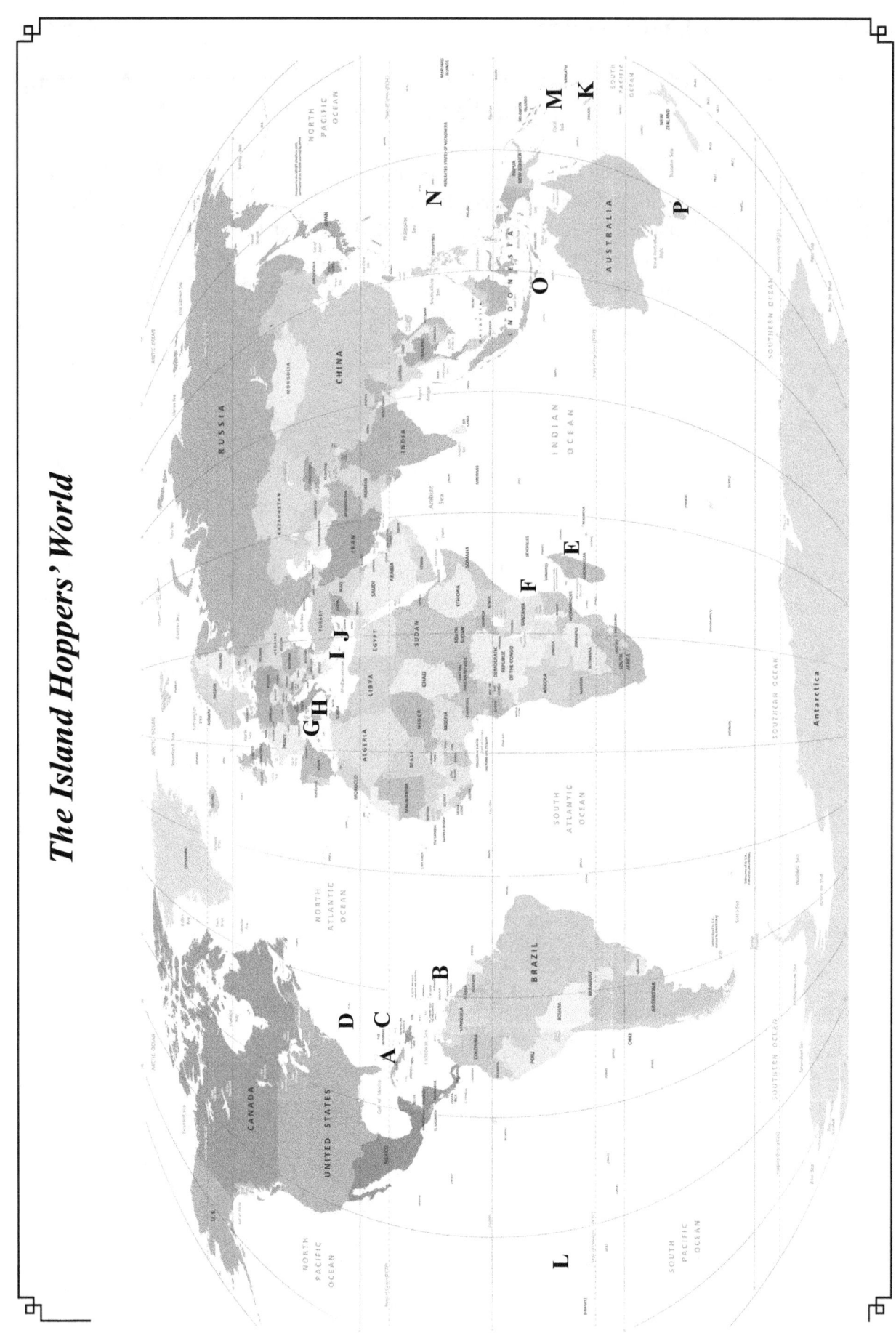

Finder Cards 1, Island Hopping *Game Cards*

Island	Your Rating	Visitors & Rating		Island	Your Rating	Visitors & Rating
Cuba	____	_____		Grenada	____	_____
Grenada	____	_____		Puerto Rico	____	_____
Rhodes	____	_____		Cyprus	____	_____
Vanuatu	____	_____		Guam	____	_____

Island	Your Rating	Visitors & Rating		Island	Your Rating	Visitors & Rating
Puerto Rico	____	_____		Bermuda	____	_____
Bermuda	____	_____		Madagascar	____	_____
Fiji	____	_____		Tahiti	____	_____
Bali	____	_____		Tasmania	____	_____

Island	Your Rating	Visitors & Rating		Island	Your Rating	Visitors & Rating
Madagascar	____	_____		Zanzibar	____	_____
Zanzibar	____	_____		Sardinia	____	_____
Rhodes	____	_____		Cyprus	____	_____
Bali	____	_____		Tasmania	____	_____

Island	Your Rating	Visitors & Rating		Island	Your Rating	Visitors & Rating
Sardinia	____	_____		Sicily	____	_____
Sicily	____	_____		Cuba	____	_____
Fiji	____	_____		Tahiti	____	_____
Vanuatu	____	_____		Guam	____	_____

Finder Cards 2, Favorite Fruits and Vegetables *Master List*

Favorite Fruits and Vegetables

You are doing a survey of your friends' favorite fruits and vegetables. On your card there are four items (your favorites). Find out who else likes these items and write their names on your card. Find one other person for each of your favorite things.

Here are the fruits and vegetables:

A. carrots

B. beets

C. squash

D. eggplant

E. spinach

F. broccoli

G. cauliflower

H. cucumbers

I. apples

J. oranges

K. grapefruit

L. grapes

M. bananas

N. pineapples

O. kiwi

P. pears

Finder Cards 2, Favorite Fruits and Vegetables   *Game Cards*

My favorites are	Friends' favorites	'My favorites are	Friends' favorites
carrots	_____	beets	_____
beets	_____	squash	_____
apples	_____	oranges	_____
bananas	_____	pineapples	_____

My favorites are	Friends' favorites	My favorites are	Friends' favorites
squash	_____	eggplant	_____
eggplant	_____	spinach	_____
grapefruit	_____	grapes	_____
kiwi	_____	pears	_____

My favorites are	Friends' favorites	My favorites are	Friends' favorites
spinach	_____	broccoli	_____
broccoli	_____	cauliflower	_____
apples	_____	oranges	_____
kiwi	_____	pears	_____

My favorites are	Friends' favorites	My favorites are	Friends' favorites
cauliflower	_____	cucumbers	_____
cucumbers	_____	carrots	_____
grapefruit	_____	grapes	_____
bananas	_____	pineapples	_____

Finder Cards 3, Vacation Spots *Master List*

Vacation Spots

On your card there are four touristic sites that you would like to visit. Find people who have the same interests and together decide on when you will visit the site and how long you will stay there.

When the game is over, one at a time tell your classmates where you will go, with whom, when, and for how long.

The master list:

A. The Grand Canyon

B. Yellowstone National Park

C. Yosemite National Park

D. Acadia National Park

E. Cape Cod National Seashore

F. The Outer Banks (North Carolina)

G. Washington, D.C.

H. Miami, Florida

I. Disneyworld at Orlando, Florida

J. Hollywood, California

K. New Orleans

L. Las Vegas

M. New England

N. Waikiki, Hawaii

O. Denali, Alaska

P. New York City

Finder Cards 3, Vacation Spots *Game Cards*

Our trip	When to go?	Stay how long?
The Grand Canyon with _____		
Yellowstone with _____	_____	_____
Disney World with _____	_____	_____
New England with _____	_____	_____
	_____	_____

Our trip	When to go?	Stay how long?
Yellowstone with _____		
Yosemite with _____	_____	_____
Hollywood with _____	_____	_____
Waikiki with _____	_____	_____
	_____	_____

Our trip	When to go?	Stay how long?
Yosemite with _____		
Acadia with _____	_____	_____
New Orleans with _____	_____	_____
Denali with _____	_____	_____
	_____	_____

Our trip	When to go?	Stay how long?
Acadia with _____		
Cape Cod with _____	_____	_____
Las Vegas with _____	_____	_____
New York City with _____	_____	_____
	_____	_____

Our trip	When to go?	Stay how long?
Cape Cod with _____		
The Outer Banks with _____	_____	_____
Disney World with _____	_____	_____
Denali with _____	_____	_____
	_____	_____

Our trip	When to go?	Stay how long?
The Outer Banks with _____		
Washington, D.C. with _____	_____	_____
Hollywood with _____	_____	_____
New York City with _____	_____	_____
	_____	_____

Our trip	When to go?	Stay how long?
Washington, D.C. with _____		
Miami with _____	_____	_____
New Orleans with _____	_____	_____
New England with _____	_____	_____
	_____	_____

Our trip	When to go?	Stay how long?
Miami with _____		
Grand Canyon with _____	_____	_____
Las Vegas with _____	_____	_____
Waikiki with _____	_____	_____
	_____	_____

Finder Cards 4, Favorite Sports *Master List*

Favorite Sports

On your card are your favorite sports. Find four others who have the same favorites. Talk about when and where you might get together to play and/or watch your favorites. At the conclusion of the game, student 1 will come to the front and identify the four people they met and what they talked about. Then student 2 comes to the front and does the same, etc.

The Master List:

A. Baseball

B. Football (American)

C. Basketball

D. Ice Hockey

E. Soccer

F. Golf

G. Tennis

H. Badminton

I. Volleyball

J. Table Tennis

K. Lacrosse

L. Field Hockey

M. Softball

N. Ten-pin Bowling

O. Ultimate Frisbee

P. Marathons

Finder Cards 4, Favorite Sports *Game Cards*

Sports When Where	**Sports** When Where
Baseball with _____ _____ _____	Football with _____ _____ _____
Football with _____ _____ _____	Basketball with _____ _____ _____
Volleyball with _____ _____ _____	Table Tennis with _____ _____ _____
Softball with _____ _____ _____	Ten-pin Bowling with _____ _____ _____

Sports When Where	**Sports** When Where
Basketball with _____ _____ _____	Ice Hockey with _____ _____ _____
Ice Hockey with _____ _____ _____	Soccer with _____ _____ _____
Lacrosse with _____ _____ _____	Field Hockey with _____ _____ _____
Ultimate Frisbee with _____ _____ _____	Marathons with _____ _____ _____

Sports When Where	**Sports** When Where
Soccer with _____ _____ _____	Golf with _____ _____ _____
Golf with _____ _____ _____	Tennis with _____ _____ _____
Volleyball with _____ _____ _____	Table Tennis with _____ _____ _____
Ultimate Frisbee with _____ _____ _____	Marathons with _____ _____ _____

Sports When Where	**Sports** When Where
Tennis with _____ _____ _____	Badminton with _____ _____ _____
Badminton with _____ _____ _____	Baseball with _____ _____ _____
Lacrosse with _____ _____ _____	Field Hockey with _____ _____ _____
Softball with _____ _____ _____	Ten-pin Bowling with _____ _____ _____

Finder Cards 5, Currency Trading *Master List*

Currency Trading

On your card you will see two currencies that you will want to sell and the price you want for them. You will also see two currencies that you want to buy and the price you want to pay. Find people who want to trade currencies with you and negotiate a price. You are doing the buying and selling in US dollars. For example you would like to get 32.8 Thai Baht for your dollar, but the seller wants to sell you fewer Baht @ 32.4 to the dollar. As the buyer, try to get more Baht.

The Currencies:

A. Thai Baht

B. Costa Rican Colon

C. Moroccan Dirham

D. Swiss Franc

E. Turkish Lira

F. Russian Ruble

G. Colombian Peso

H. Mexican Peso

I. Brazilian Real

J. Saudi Arabian Riyal

K. Indian Rupee

L. Israeli Shekel

M. South Korean Won

N. Japanese Yen

O. Chinese Yuan Renminbi

P. Polish Zloty

Finder Cards 5, Currency Trading *Game Cards*

	Buy	Sell
Thai Baht	@ 32.8	
Costa Rican Colon	@ 550	
Mexican Peso		@ 15.5
Polish Zloty		@ 3.85

	Buy	Sell
Moroccan Dirham	10.5	
Swiss Franc	@ 0.98	
Thai Baht		@ 32.4
Brazilian Real		@ 3.0

	Buy	Sell
Turkish Lira	@ 2.9	
Russian Ruble	@ 55	
Costa Rican Colon		@ 530
Saudi Arabian Riyal		@ 3.75

	Buy	Sell
Colombian Peso	@ 2,500	
Mexican Peso	@ 15.25	
Moroccan Dirham		@ 9.9
Indian Rupee		@ 63.0

	Buy	Sell
Brazilian Real	@ 3.25	
Saudi Arabian Riyal	@ 3.85	
Swiss Franc		@ 0.95
Israeli Shekel		@ 3.9

	Buy	Sell
Indian Rupee	@ 65.0	
Israeli Shekel	@ 4.2	
Turkish Lira		@ 2.7
South Korean Won		@ 1,081

	Buy	Sell
South Korean Won	@ 1,100	
Japanese Yen	@ 125	
Russian Ruble		@ 53.0
Chinese Yuan Reminbi		@ 6.2

	Buy	Sell
Chinese Yuan Reminbi	@ 6.4	
Polish Zloty	@ 3.9	
Japanese Yen		@ 120
Colombian Peso		@ 2,480

Finder Cards 6, Timeshare Swap *Game Cards*

Timeshare Swap

Teacher Notes. Not all these cards will result in a match. The following are matches: 1 and 4, 5 and 8, 9 and 12; 13 and 16; 17 and 20. Use the cards in the order of their numbers. Mix them thoroughly as you hand them out. If you have more than 20 students, have some students double up as partners.

For the student. Summer is coming and you "own" a timeshare in a condo. This year you would like to swap your place for another place whose owner would like to stay in your place. For example, you have a timeshare in New Orleans and you want to find someone who has a timeshare in Sedona and would like to swap places with you for the same dates. WARNING: You may not be successful.

Timeshare 1
You own a condo in Chicago
You want to swap with San Francisco
Your dates: 10/15-30

Timeshare 2
You own a condo in San Francisco
You want to swap with Chicago
Your dates: 9/15-30

Timeshare 3
You own a condo in San Francisco
You want swap with Chicago
Your dates: 5/15-30

Timeshare 4
You own a condo in San Francisco
You want swap with Chicago
Your dates: 10/15-30

Timeshare 5
You own a condo in Seattle
You want to swap with Bermuda
Your dates: 3/1-15

Timeshare 6
You own a condo in Bermuda
You want to swap with Seattle
Your dates: 4/1-15

Timeshare 7
You own a condo in Bermuda
You want to swap with Seattle
Your dates: 6/1-15

Timeshare 8
You own a condo in Bermuda
You want to swap with Seattle
Your dates: 3/1-15

Finder Cards 6, Timeshare Swap *Game Cards*

Timeshare 9

You own a condo in New Orleans
You want to swap with Sedona
Your dates: 7/14-28

Timeshare 10

You own a condo in Sedona
You want to swap with New Orleans
Your dates: 7/7-21

Timeshare 11

You own a condo in Sedona
You want to swap with New Orleans
Your dates: 12/20-30

Timeshare 12

You own a condo in Sedona
You want to swap with New Orleans
Your dates: 7/14-28

Timeshare 13

You own a condo in Cape Cod
You want to swap with Miami
Your dates: 4/15-30

Timeshare 14

You own a condo in Miami
You want to swap with Cape Cod
Your dates: 4/1-15

Timeshare 15

You own a condo in Miami
You want to swap with Cape Cod
Your dates: 6/10-24

Timeshare 16

You own a condo in Miami
You want to swap with Cape Cod
Your dates: 4/15-30

Timeshare 17

You own a condo in Las Vegas
You want to swap with Dallas
Your dates: 10/15 - 30

Timeshare 18

You own a condo in Dallas
You want to swap with Las Vegas
Your dates: 2/7-21

Timeshare 19

You own a condo in Dallas
You want to swap with Las Vegas
Your dates: 7/1-14

Timeshare 20

You own a condo in Dallas
You want to swap with Las Vegas
Your dates: 10/15-30

Used Auto Buying and Selling

Teacher Notes. This activity is set up for 8 students. It can be played with fewer students, but in that case some students may not be able to buy or sell one of their cars. For best results, us the cards in order from the top, left to right, i.e. cards A – D. Or you can have some student have two cards. With more than 8 students, you can have some work as "partners."

For the student. You will have either a seller card or a buyer card. Sellers will try people who will buy their cars, while buyers will try to find people who will sell them the car they want.

The Cars:

a. Ford Focus

b. Ford Fusion

c. Chevrolet Camaro

d. Chevrolet Cruze

e. Hyundai Tucson

f. Hyundai Santa Fe

g. Toyota RAV 4

h. Toyota Prius

i. Volkswagen Jetta

j. Volkswagen Beetle

k. Kia Sorento

l. Kia Sportage

m. Nissan Altima

n. Nissan Acura

o. Subaru Forester

p. Subaru Impreza

Seller A

You want to sell:

- Ford Focus
- Ford Fusion
- Volkswagen Jetta
- Volkswagen Beetle

Buyer A

You want to buy:

- Subaru Forester
- Ford Focus
- Chevrolet Camaro
- Nissan Acura

Seller B

You want to sell:

- Chevrolet Camaro
- Chevrolet Cruze
- Kia Sorento
- Kia Sportage

Buyer B

You want to buy:

- Nissan Altima
- Ford Fusion
- Chevrolet Cruze
- Subaru Impreza

Seller C

You want to sell:

- Hyundai Tucson
- Hyundai Santa Fe
- Nissan Altima
- Nissan Acura

Buyer C

You want to buy:

- Kia Sorento
- Hyundai Tucson
- Toyota Prius
- Volkswagen Beetle

Seller D

You want to sell:

- Toyota RAV 4
- Toyota Prius
- Subaru Forester
- Subaru Impreza

Buyer D

You want to buy:

- Volkswagen Jetta
- Toyota RAV 4
- Hyundai Santa Fe
- Kia Sportage

APPENDIX

Phonetic Spelling Key

Sound	Example	Sound	Example
A	CAT	N	NAG
AI	KATE	NG	SANG
AH	COT	O	NO
AY	KITE	OO	NEW
AW	BALL	OU	NOW
B	BAT	OY	BOY
CH	CHAT	P	PAT
D	DAD	R	RAT
E	BET	S	SAT
EE	BEET	SH	SHOW
ER	BERRY	T	TOY
er	BETTER	TH	THAT
F	FAT	th	THIN
G	GAT	U	TOOK
H	HAT	UH	ABOVE
HW	WHICH	uh	ABOVE
I	BIT	V	VAT
J	JACK	W	WITCH
K	CAN	Y	YET
L	LAD	Z	ZEN
M	MAD	ZH	MEASURE